NATIONAL IDENTITY AND EUROPE

EUROPEAN MEDIA MONOGRAPHS

Series editor: Richard Paterson

Already published:

After The Wall: Broadcasting in Germany
edited by Geoffrey Nowell-Smith and Tana Wollen

Forthcoming titles:

*Wires or Wireless: The Convergence of Broadcasting
and Telecommunications in Europe*
Nicholas Garnham

Media Law and Regulation in Europe
Wulf Meinel

Winner Takes All: The Resistible Rise of Silvio Berlusconi
Waddick Doyle

EUROPEAN MEDIA MONOGRAPHS

NATIONAL IDENTITY AND EUROPE

The Television Revolution

Edited by
Phillip Drummond, Richard Paterson and Janet Willis

BFI Publishing

First published in 1993 by the
British Film Institute
21 Stephen Street
London W1P 1PL

© British Film Institute 1993

British Library Cataloguing in Publication Data

National Identity and Europe:
Television Revolution. – (European Media Monographs)
   I. Drummond, Phillip   II. Series
   384.55094

ISBN 0–85170–382–8

Cover design: Geoff Wiggins

Typeset in 10 on 11½pt Plantin by
Fakenham Photosetting Ltd
Fakenham, Norfolk
Printed in Great Britain by
St Edmundsbury Press
Bury St Edmunds, Suffolk

Contents

Acknowledgments

The Fourth International Television Studies Conference, from which the papers in this volume were drawn, was held in London in July 1991. It was made possible by the time, energy and material support of many people and institutions whose contribution we wish to acknowledge.

Both the British Film Institute Research Division and the University of London Institute of Education's Department of English and Media Studies have maintained their consistent long-term support. In addition, sponsorship from the Hōsō-Bunka Foundation, UNESCO, the British Council, the Ford Foundation, the Bouverie Trust and Channel Four enabled a broad range of speakers from more than thirty countries to attend and to participate in lively intellectual debate and social celebration.

We wish to thank a number of individuals for their support to the conference. In particular, we would like to record our gratitude to Anthony Smith, President of Magdalen College, Oxford, who has had a long association with the Conference and who, in addition to acting as Honorary President, alongside Professor Stuart Hall, delivered the first Hilde Himmelweit Memorial Lecture. The Conference benefited over a number of years from Professor Himmelweit's imaginative and powerful support even as she coped bravely with her illness, and Anthony Smith's lecture was a fitting tribute. We were supported both in the preparation and realisation of the Conference by the invaluable assistance of an Advisory Committee: David Buckingham, Ed Buscombe, Richard Collins, Thérèse Daniels, David Docherty, Bob Ferguson, Ivor Gaber, Barrie Gunter, Bronwen Maddox, Robin McGregor, Geoffrey Nowell-Smith, Duncan Petrie, Chris Richards and Tana Wollen. We would also like to thank the postgraduate media students of the Institute of Education who took on the role of Conference stewards. Their energy and cheerfulness added much to the smooth running of a large and complicated event.

We also warmly thank Elaine Randall, Jacintha Cusack and Anita Miller at the BFI and Ann Doyle of the Institute of Education for their magnificent work over many months, and their help in making the Conference such a success. Finally, we again record our thanks to all those speakers, chairpersons and delegates from around the world who participated in the continuing excitement of defining and redefining the field of television studies.

PHILLIP DRUMMOND
RICHARD PATERSON
Executive Directors, ITSC 1991

JANET WILLIS
Director, ITSC 1991

Contributors

Pavel Campeanu: Executive Director, Independent Centre for Social and Opinion Studies; Professor, Political Sociology, the International Department, University of Bucharest, Romania.

Marie Gillespie: Lecturer, Sociology of Communication Department, Brunel University.

Alison Griffiths: PhD student and Research Assistant, Department of Cinema Studies, New York University.

Stig Hjarvard: Research Fellow, Department of Film and Media Studies, University of Copenhagen.

Breda Luthar: Assistant, Theory of Mass Communication course, Department of Journalism, Faculty of Social Sciences, University of Ljubljana, Slovenia.

Toby Miller: Lecturer, Communication Studies, Murdoch University, Australia.

Sergei Muratov: Senior Lecturer, Department of Television, Faculty of Journalism, Moscow State University.

Vincent Porter: Professor, Centre for Communication and Information Studies, University of Westminster.

Eduard Sagalayev: President, Moscow Independent Broadcasting Company, former director of Ostankino Television Company.

Daphne Skillen: Honorary Visiting Fellow, School of Slavonic and East European Studies, University of London.

Editors

Phillip Drummond: Executive Director, International Television Studies Conference 1991. Director, MA Media Programme, University of London Institute of Education.

Richard Paterson: Executive Director, International Television Studies Conference 1991. Deputy Head, Research Division; Head of Communications Group, BFI.

Janet Willis: Director, International Television Studies Conference 1991. Research Projects Officer, Television and Projects Unit, BFI.

Introduction
Collective Identity, Television and Europe

Television has witnessed and participated in the massive resurgence of questions of national identity throughout Europe in recent years. The precise ways in which it has contributed to these far-reaching social changes remain open to analysis. Collective identities are of course complex in their formation and have an existence which is prior to their expression through the medium of television. But television has played various roles, however subordinate, in the business of negotiating the profound social, political and cultural changes in Europe, and, given its near-universal availability, seems destined to continue to have a role of significance.

This collection of essays, drawn from the Fourth International Television Studies Conference held in London in 1991, is concerned both with television and with the processes by which collective identity is defined and changed. Collective identity is approached here from a number of different concerns, and, importantly, from within a variety of 'national' perspectives. This anthology moves beyond the broad speculative thrust of much earlier work and is grounded in an empirical detail which confirms the need for a much deeper theoretical perspective from across the range of disciplines. This approach to questions of collective identity in television studies began to emerge at ITSC 1988 but became more prominent both in the 1991 conference and, more spectacularly, in the real world.

For this collection we have chosen essays which concentrate on specific instances of identity formation within the larger local/global opposition. The essays in the first section deal broadly with the use of television among particular ethnic communities in Europe in a range of political and cultural circumstances. The second section includes consideration of European supra-national issues, impinging on wider international trade and legal agreements which have effects on national policies for film and television. The third section concerns television involvement in the collapsing Soviet bloc, and provides a case-study background to this important moment in European history.

Television's contribution in this extraordinary period can be analysed *inter alia* through its influence on policy outcomes, in terms of the questions of representation and citizenship, and in terms of audience response to producers' intentional interpretative acts. The audience's complex reaction to what is offered, partially structured by the parameters and processes of the socio-political milieu, remains a central factor in understanding and analysing the relationship of collective identities and television.

Questions of Identity
Analysis of 'identity' during the 1980s concentrated largely on important questions concerning racial difference in European states and the manifestations of and counteractions towards racism. The possibility of creating a European identity and the discourse of Europeanism continued to attract the attention of politicians and commentators as the European Community grew in influence and strength. The importance of the ethnic communities in European states began to take a particularly nationalistic inflection in the late 1980s, even though it had never completely disappeared from the political discourse in nations-without-states (Scotland, Catalonia etc.) across Europe. Europe was surprised to witness the re-emergence of old grievances as the political changes in Eastern and Central Europe returned older identity formations to the nexus of everyday politics, leading to sometimes violent inter-ethnic conflicts. This resurgent 'identity politics' and burgeoning nationalisms have unknown consequences across Europe and for the larger European Community project.

What is at stake is the fundamental question concerning the very definition of Europe and of those who are seen to have a European identity. The notion of identity itself, in many spheres, is defined by otherness. It acts together with questions of territoriality and collective representations which might encompass heroes, memories, thought styles. There is a series of shared classifications which elicit and sustain the individual's (and group's) commitment to the social order.[1] The central task is to explain this general question of the individual's commitment to the social order, as Durkheim insisted. His solution was to look to the shared classifications which underpin solidarity and collective action. This can be contrasted to Weber's concentration on the impact of particular ideas at particular stages of institutional analysis, or to a Kantian or Humean emphasis on individual self-determination. The tension between these positions can be seen to operate across political and cultural discourses, and different versions of television studies, too, pay allegiance to these analytical differences. In short, what is the role of the individual?

Each individual has a complexity of identities. One analysis sees the domains of identity of the individual as a series of concentric points of reference whereby individuals participate in many different intersecting circles, none of which can command their individual allegiance. The individual may enjoy a different status and perhaps even a different identity in each of them, with the result that instability and personal insecurity become the norm.[2] This analysis, however, ignores the emotional charge associated with nationalism and cannot explain the responsiveness to new labels which suggests an extraordinary readiness to fall into new slots and to let selfhood be redefined.[3] It is unable to explain the re-emergence of historically buried antagonisms and oppositions based on modes of identification.

On the broader political front we should consider Anthony D. Smith's definition of national identity which separates a 'Western' from a non-Western model. In this framework the fundamental features of national identity include a historical territory or homeland; common myths and historical memories; a common, mass public culture; common legal rights and duties for all members; and a common economy with territorial mobility for members. Smith distinguishes the 'Western' model by its foundation in law and rights, which in the ethnic, non-Western model is overshadowed by vernacular culture, including language and custom.[4]

For Smith, changes in collective identities are often based on traumatic developments which 'disturb the basic patterning of the cultural elements that make up the sense of continuity, shared memories and notions of collective destiny.'[5] His view should be considered against the reality of television practices, be they at the level of policy or of programme-making. What it offers is a context for analysis of the changes taking place in Europe which can be applied to case studies of television production.

For intellectuals or for television producers in Europe there are tensions between the national, the ambition of the supranational institutions (with its baggage carried by multinational capital, but also by public service-oriented pan-European organisations) and the different ethnic dimensions. It is important both analytically and politically to include groups identifiable by difference within terri-

3

torial boundaries of the state, as well as the re-emergent ethnic communities. The Council of Europe, and latterly the EC too in some of its pronouncements, has offered policies based on the notion of diversity with unity – but such unity can have racist overtones, as revealed in Johan Galtung's analysis. It is about exclusion and inclusion at the same time.[6] Sameness is not a quality that can be recognised in things themselves; it is conferred within a coherent scheme. Recognition, in this sense, implies exclusion and the drawing of boundaries.

The European Case
We would propose that the study of identities, or of processes of identification, needs to proceed in two distinct, but complementary, directions where television studies are concerned. Firstly, it should work 'top down' – analysing the discourses of 'nation' offered in the governmentalisation of the state. States are based on a knowable and governable economic and social space in which populations are seen as objects of knowledge. Understanding these classificatory frameworks requires an understanding of the discursive formations emanating from institutions at all levels, a sense of how institutions think. In television it is necessary to focus *inter alia* on the role of the medium as discursive carrier and television's specificity within the social formation. Second, we need to proceed 'bottom up' – in particular, in television studies, through the analysis of how individuals negotiate programme output. At both levels, clearly, this requires analysis of the cultural mission embodied by the very existence of particular institutions. In both types of analysis, broader perspectives which locate the process in time and space need to be deployed. The important historical analyses by Febvre and Martin in *The Coming of the Book*, and Braudel's *The Mediterranean and the Mediterranean World in the Age of Philip II*, are suggestive in placing communications media centre-stage in the unfolding drama of identity and politics.

The return, or creation, of 'national' traditions in the folkloristic mode of television programming – in, for instance, the new states within the former Yugoslavia or Soviet Union – must repay close analysis. Breda Luthar's paper begins to approach these questions in its analysis of the Slovenian version of a game show entitled *She and He*. As Ernest Gellner intimates, nationalism sometimes takes preexisting cultures and turns them into nations, sometimes invents them, and often obliterates them.[7] Alison Griffiths's essay reviews the specificity of audience reaction and responses to the Welsh-language soap opera *Pobol y Cwm*, and the redefinition and celebration of national and cultural identity. Again a complex picture emerges of identity negotiation in and through television viewing.

Marie Gillespie's ethnographic work on a young Punjabi audience's interpretations of the Australian soap opera *Neighbours* shows how their viewing experiences are woven into the fabric of everyday life; how they are negotiated through their specific concerns in the London suburb where they live; and identifies the cultural specificity of life in Punjabi families. Her essay both confirms a radical constructivism in the appropriation of TV texts by audiences, and shows how specific cultural traits are deployed in the interpretations. These essays underline, once more, the need for a knowledge of context in understanding modes of identification.

The still more fundamental question – what is Europe? – continues to return in ever more persistent form. At one level of contemporary politics it is defined by Article 8 of the Treaty on European Union. In our modern polity it involves questions of rights and of citizenship; it suggests, by implication, that representations are fair. There is, however, no simple articulation of representativeness inside the media, let alone in the political field. Much of the work of the European Court of Human Rights and of the European Court of Justice can be understood in terms of achieving this baseline in case law. Here Vincent Porter's essay usefully broaches the clash of the opposing discourses of commercial and citizen interests in recent human rights judgments on the media in Europe, taking the emerging broadcasting pluralism in Germany, France and Ireland as key examples.

Moreover, the politics of the trade in television and its associated discourses fit uneasily with a goal of cultural diversity. Definitions of a Europe of nations have to be debated in the light of possible European union, the discourse of Europeanism, and – for television – addressed through the terms of the 'Television Without Frontiers' directive. Here organisational questions emerge as well, as Stig Hjarvard shows in his essay detailing the rationale behind the EBU's support for a Europe-wide news channel, Euronews.

Institutions survive by harnessing all information processes to the task of establishing themselves. Industrial and state groups push for particular solutions which may be denied by 'consumer' realities. European legislation organises public debate and imposes a degree of certainty on uncertainty by delivering a harmonised framework of shared classifications.

The HD-MAC format of high-definition television is an interesting example of an industrial product – developed in response to a perceived trade threat, underpinned by 'European' institutions –

5

whose fate is out of line with the different national ambitions within the supra-national community. Japan is identified as threat to justify research and development, just as American culture remains both defining and 'other' for European television culture. The global questions which are implied in the struggle for industrial supremacy, and are reflected in Toby Miller's essay on GATT and questions of the traded image in national policy decisions, further emphasise the European polity's difficulties.

The media *are* a battlefield, and in Europe a complex play of strategy and counter-strategy is involved.[8] The media are implicated at the level of trade, of national and global pressures, of perceived threats (often couched in historical terms), and within the framework of law and rights. The possibility of transnational TV, now a reality through satellite, comes up against the fundamental questions of a diffuse policy process and the need for a social contract between viewer (as citizen as well as consumer) and broadcaster under the regulatory gaze of the democratic polity, where such exists.

One connecting analytical thread for this study of television's changing role in Europe is that of viewer identity and viewer perception of programming. The Christian definition of Europe positions otherness. Television's relation to the narrative traditions of the West, already deeply implicated in Christianity, acts as carrier of prevailing norms. Against the grain there are some attempts to broaden representation and to recognise the cosmopolitan nature of society in a Europe in its post-colonial phase. Television can be seen as proactive in these circumstances, just as it could be seen as a means of cementing and bonding national consensus in the Britain of the 50s and 60s.[9] Any institution starts to control the memory of its members and provides the categories of their thought, sets the terms for self-knowledge, and fixes identities.[10] Europe in flux relies on television as information source to carry and amplify ideas for future development. Much is said about the democratic deficit in the ever-growing European Community. The role of television, and the goodwill and noble sentiments attaching to its development, is in some ways more complex than perhaps imagined, but crucial to the next phase of change. Questions of cohesion, of territoriality and boundaries, of the tensions produced by the perception of an over-centralised super-state, are mediated through and possibly partially formed by television's representations. The congruence of culture and polity is most apparent and powerful within television, but how central the place of media is in nation-state cohesion is open to debate.[11]

These conflicting views necessitate an extension of our analytical framework in the face of the march of history. This collection of essays reflects directly the far-reaching changes in European broadcasting in the early 1990s. At one level television can probably be no more than a witness to these extraordinary events. We have included the accounts of Pavel Campeanu, Sergei Muratov and Eduard Sagalayev both for this reason and because they begin to map out the complex involvement of television in any social and political revolution. Campeanu illustrates the prefiguration of Romania's revolution in television viewing habits, and television's function as part of the mechanism of restructuring. The papers from the former Soviet Union are included to indicate the direction of thinking there just before the attempted coup of August 1991 and the collapse of the old regime and its structures. The brave sentiments reflected in the moves towards an independent media system, in that period of increasing repression and uncertainty, are all the more interesting in the light of Daphne Skillen's account of subsequent changes in Russian media.

Conclusion

In recent years, on the one hand we have seen the move towards the single European market and wider European union, on the other a rapid disintegration of the communist bloc, culminating in the fragmentation of Yugoslavia and the Soviet Union. Subsequent events have reinforced this pattern of fragmentation as the Balkan states have returned to a condition of tension and conflict. It is difficult to escape a growing suspicion of the 'south' in the 'north' of Europe. Islam is seen by some as the alien at the gate. Even what constitutes the north is becoming a political question, as the success of the Lombardy League in Italy shows and as a growing scepticism emerges concerning the role of Greece in the European Community. The future for Europe and its peoples is clouded in doubt. Television in the coming years must remain as a conduit of information, openly accountable inside a democratic order. Within that framework the identities we decide to inhabit will change as we adapt to the processes of yet new circumstances. Television will not change the course of history, but nor will it be innocent in these momentous days.

Richard Paterson

Notes

1. See Emile Durkheim, *The Rules of Sociological Method* (New York: Free Press, 1964); Mary Douglas, *How Institutions Think* (London: Rout-

7

ledge and Kegan Paul, 1987); Maurice Halbwachs, *The Collective Memory* (New York: Harper & Row, 1980; originally published as *La mémoire collective*, Paris: Presses Universitaires de France, 1950); Philip Schlesinger, *Media, State and Nation* (London: Sage, 1991).

2. Louis Wirth, 'Urbanism as a Way of Life', *American Journal of Sociology*, vol. 44, 1938, pp. 1–24. Cf. Alberto Melucci, *Nomads of the Present* (London: Hutchinson Radius, 1989).

3. Cf. Douglas, *How Institutions Think*, p. 100.

4. Anthony D. Smith, *National Identity* (London: Penguin, 1991); Ernest Gellner, *Nations and Nationalism* (Oxford: Basil Blackwell, 1983), pp. 97–109 *passim* on nationalism, the nation-state and culture.

5. Smith, *National Identity*, p. 12.

6. See Johan Galtung, *Europe in the Making* (New York: Crane Russak, 1989); and, for a wider perspective, William Wallace (ed.), *The Dynamics of European Integration* (London: Pinter/Royal Institute of International Affairs, 1990), p. 161.

7. Gellner, *Nations and Nationalism*, p. 48.

8. See Philip Schlesinger, 'Media, the Political Order and National Identity', *Media, Culture and Society*, vol. 13 no. 3, July 1991.

9. See *Report of the Committee on Broadcasting 1960* (The Pilkington Report), Cmnd. 1753 (London: HMSO, 1962).

10. Douglas, *How Institutions Think*, p. 70.

11. Cf. K. Deutsch, *Nationalism and Social Communication: an Inquiry into the Foundation of Nationality* (2nd edition, Cambridge, Mass.: MIT Press, 1966), and Gellner, *Nations and Nationalism*.

Pobol y Cwm

The Construction of National and Cultural Identity in a Welsh-Language Soap Opera

Alison Griffiths

Introduction

This essay arises out of a growing interest in the popular Welsh-language soap opera *Pobol y Cwm* and the extent to which the pleasure it gives to a large number of viewers derives from its Welsh discourse and definitions of cultural and national identity. Welsh-language broadcasting has been largely neglected in debates surrounding popular culture and pleasure in the 1970s and 80s; the Welsh-language text has been excluded and marginalised from English-language academic research, with little translated Welsh-language material being made available. Documented evidence of research into the study of Welsh identity in popular televisual forms is extremely scarce. Furthermore, critics are generally quick to deride pleasurable Welsh-language genres for their low production values and/or anglicised discourse.[1]

Attention in this essay will therefore focus on the ideological 'effect' of *Pobol y Cwm* in offering definitions and re-definitions of 'Welshness' and contributing to (re)formations of cultural identity. By cultural identity, I refer to codified systems and ideological forms that contribute to the sense of a collective experience based on a range of shared assumptions and ideas. The main areas of investigation are structured around four key concerns: firstly, the social, cultural and institutional forms of *Pobol y Cwm* and their role in defining and positioning the soap within a Welsh discourse (this section also includes consideration of the role of culture in contributing to a sense of Welsh identity, and frames the discourse of *Pobol y Cwm* against representations of other UK nations); secondly, analysis of textual ideologies visible in the soap with specific focus on a controversial storyline; thirdly, the role of *Pobol y Cwm* in the lives

9

of its young viewers and their understanding of ideological concerns; and, finally, the future of popular genres in Welsh-language broadcasting in the light of deregulation and new technologies.

Social, Cultural and Institutional Forms

The Welsh language distinguishes Wales as a country within both the United Kingdom and a broader European community. In recent years it has enjoyed a modest yet significant revival, boosted by its status as a core National Curriculum subject in Welsh-language schools and a foundation subject in all other schools. The language is unquestionably the foundation upon which Welsh culture and sense of national identity resides; many 'characteristics' and definitions of Wales have been constructed around the language, which acts as a reaffirmation of Wales' autonomy.

Wales has two distinct dialectical forms of the language, one form situated in the north, the other in the south. Since the growth of various media institutions in Wales, and particularly since the introduction of S4C, the differences in sound and expression have meant that each form of the language has striven for national recognition as the superior paradigm. Thus the difference between the North and the South Walean is often viewed in comic terms in popular culture, with numerous reworkings of stereotypical traits.

Since its inception, *Pobol y Cwm* has been a soap opera broadcast in the Welsh language. To the non Welsh-speaking viewer, it is a foreign language as strange and alien as any other small-nation discourse. However, just as other UK soap operas are positioned in localities with distinct though frequently contrived and romanticised discourses and dialects, so *Pobol y Cwm* is firmly situated in a region of Wales characterised by a specific linguistic mode and rural diegesis.

In an attempt to bridge the gap caused by the dialectical divide and to attract North Walean viewers, there are a few North Walean characters in *Pobol y Cwm*, though it is interesting to note that the most prominent of these, Meic Pierce, a local café owner, is a comic character and frequently the butt of humorous storylines. Gwyn Hughes-Jones (producer, 1988–89) admits that the north/south mix is an unrealistic device as small west Wales villages seldom, if ever, have North and South Waleans sharing the community. Despite lacking in realism, however, it does contribute to the soap's broad appeal across the Principality.

Another device used to attract a different type of audience, the Welsh-language learner, has been used in previous series. A young couple, a Breton wife and her English-speaking husband, were introduced into the soap when they bought a smallholding on the fringes of the community. Determined to learn the language and integrate into the community, the couple were treated sympathetically by the locals of Cwmderi and not as outsiders (the more obvious choice of storyline). The producers were anxious, however, not to restrict the characters in terms of their diegetic function as 'Welsh-language learners'. Instead, they were keen to explore by means of drama the issue of integration through language acquisition, and in so doing develop a unique soap opera discourse. The Lloyds, therefore, represent a progressive storyline that is able to explore the question of integration and the role language can play in breaking down barriers. As a transmitter of culture, the Welsh-language discourse of *Pobol y Cwm* is thus capable of inspiring innovative storylines, and addressing the notion of language as a symbol of cultural identity.

Humour has always occupied a prominent position in the discourse of *Pobol y Cwm*. Every small nation and region believes it has developed its own idiosyncratic style and form of humour. The Liverpool paradigm received considerable media attention with the success of 'alternative' comedian Alexei Sayle in the 1980s, though it had been recognised much earlier in, for instance, the long-running sitcom *The Liver Birds*. The black comedy *Boys from the Blackstuff* was highly acclaimed both for its social and political commentary on the effects of unemployment and for its razor-sharp humour. The film *Letter to Brezhnev* also popularised Scouse humour. The ubiquitous Liverpudlian accent and style of humour characterised many youth programmes and remains a distinctive feature of the successful soap *Brookside*.

The form of Welsh humour contained in the discourse of *Pobol y Cwm* derives, on the one hand, from the classic gossip/inquisitive nature of many rural village people, and on the other, from the slightly macabre rugby club culture. It could be argued, however, that the former is less a distinctive *cultural* feature and more a formulaic device and character type found in almost all popular British soaps: Dot Cotton in *EastEnders*; Hilda Ogden and now Vera Duckworth in *Coronation Street*; and to a certain extent Harry Cross in *Brookside*.

The *Pobol y Cwm* production team firmly believe that humour should occupy a protected and privileged position in the programme's remit. Humour, in fact, plays a significant role institutionally. At a storylining meeting attended by this author, ideas and thematic developments considered by the producer, senior script editor and two resident scriptwriters were constantly injected with

11

comic overtones; the whole mood of the meeting was relaxed, with humorous quips and asides featuring regularly in the conversation.

As a consequence of this policy, entertainment becomes the medium through which issues are raised and explored in the soap. This was apparent in the launch of the 'invasion' storyline that examined the effect of non-sympathetic English immigration into the area. Ron Unsworth, an ex-Birmingham landlord, had accepted the tenancy of a local village pub, 'The Farmers' Arms', a once quiet and traditional place which Ron planned to modernise through introducing gimmicks such as a 'Happy Hour' and Sunday morning striptease shows. Much of the humour resided in the clash of cultures: Ron's brash, 'urbanised' temperament, in opposition to the locals' bemused, unassuming response. The nub of this humour emerges in a joke two of the locals play on Ron. One of them pretends he cannot speak English as he was brought up by his 'bible-thumping grandmother on a farm in the mountain', never went to school, and subsequently could only speak Welsh. Ron is amazed by this story, though believes it to be true. In the ensuing dialogue, the two locals use many Welsh stereotypes to fuel and sustain the humour – religion; unpronounceable Welsh names; uncivilised existence; the stupidity of the Welsh figure 'Taffy' etc. The self-denigrating device is quintessentially Welsh, and found frequently in comic interchanges in the series. Unfortunately, much of the humour is linguistically specific and therefore lost in the subtitled translation for non-Welsh-speaking viewers. The scene is nevertheless ideologically loaded with references to perceived Welsh and English stereotypes.

The decision to produce and broadcast on the same day offered the production team of *Pobol y Cwm* a unique facility: a sense of immediacy unparalleled in British soap opera. Unlike the three other major soaps, which operate a policy of shooting material to be broadcast in 4–6 weeks, *Pobol y Cwm* could introduce significant national and regional non-diegetic references, albeit in a referential form, whilst recording a particular day's episode.

An example arose in a December 1988 episode which was to be broadcast the evening after the Lockerbie air disaster. Great concern was expressed as to the form any reference to the disaster should take. An attempt to incorporate this horrific incident in thirty seconds air-time could inadvertently trivialise it, particularly if the remainder of the episode was humorous. Eventually a decision was made to shoot the beginning of that day's episode with a close-up of the landlord of the local pub gazing at the front page of a national newspaper. The scene was played in absolute silence, with the camera pulling back to reveal the landlord's shocked and saddened expression. The producer believed the scene was most effective in conveying a sense of horror and loss without sensationalising the incident. With the disturbing regularity of national 'disasters', however, incidents are examined carefully and will not automatically receive coverage.

An area that does attract fairly regular topical reference during the season is the game of rugby. In the 1988–89 season Wales had fared dreadfully in all their matches and were facing the 'wooden spoon' unless they were victorious against England in the last match of the five-nations tournament, to be played at Cardiff Arms Park. A pub scene during Friday's episode focused entirely on the outcome of the match, and how national pride was at stake, particularly when playing against England. The subsequent victory and commentary on the match were discussed in the pub in Monday's episode. Despite the enormous benefits of this facility in contributing to the sense of realism and 'unrecorded existence' of *Pobol y Cwm*, the producer is well aware of the importance of balance: the soap is not a news information programme, but is concerned with the day-to-day lives of its characters and aspects of their existence and identities.

The Role of Culture in Defining Identity
The three small nations that together with England make up the United Kingdom have been represented in multifarious forms on national television since the early 1950s. However, critics have argued that professionals engaged in producing programmes in Wales are encouraged merely to reproduce dominant 'UK' mainstream broadcasting values through the Welsh language.[2] Furthermore, the main concern of the 'white, middle-class elite' who run the broadcasting institutions in Wales has been to preserve all that is traditional in Welsh culture, secure in the knowledge that such a policy will not compromise their allegiance to and security within the British Establishment.[3]

The form of this relationship, together with the effects this 'marriage' has had on the programme content and dominant representations of Scottish television, has been discussed by Colin McArthur. He believes that there has been a certain pressure on Scottish television producers to privilege an image of Scotland that is widely marketable. Moreover, just as British television is increasingly dependent on the kinds of dramatisation and serialisation which will attract co-production finance and international sales, so Scottish television looks for financial and prestigious approval to London and the independent network. The result is a marketable image of Scotland that confirms rather than challenges the dominant discourse of 'Scottishness'.[4]

One of the gross inadequacies of Scottish television for McArthur, therefore, is the absence of any sense of engagement with a developed notion of national culture or national identity which goes beyond the reflection of an always already constructed 'Scottishness': 'It is in its lack of engagement, rather than in the sense of good or bad programmes, that Scottish television is at best inadequate, at worst inimical to the development of Scottish culture.'[5] This criticism is frequently levelled in the Welsh context at *Pobol y Cwm*. Opponents attack the soap for its presumed lack of engagement with any progressive notion of 'Welshness', arguing that *Pobol y Cwm* is content to reproduce dominant, 'safe', tried and tested forms of representation that are regressive and vacuous.

Absent from these critiques, however, is any form of *real* engagement with the soap or consideration of its generic conventions and popular pleasure. Critics seldom refer directly to the text and are content to make judgments frequently based on their memory of the 'old-style' format. Moreover, what might a progressive Welsh cultural identity look like if discovered, and what exactly do we mean by the terms 'progressive' and 'culture'?

Developing from definitions of culture which appeared in the 1950s and 1960s through the work of E. P. Thompson, Raymond Williams and Richard Hoggart, the role of a Welsh national culture would be to provide points of identification around which individuals or groups could discover or recognise their 'Welshness', a Welshness which can then be held together as a special and unique identity in the face of the pressures towards nationless and classless homogeneity.[6] In applying this model to 'Scottishness', John Caughie argues that such a view exists in regressive and progressive forms: in its regressive forms national culture becomes the 'celebration of national identity, a national identity which is always already given'; while in its progressive forms, it is concerned with 'positive images, with the establishment by discovery or recovery of ... identity and traditions which can be mobilised as the basis for political action'.[7]

This notion of an 'already given identity' is a particularly interesting polemic to apply to the paradigm of 'Welshness' and the role of Welsh television in defining and contributing to a national culture. McArthur argues that the discourses of Tartanry and Kailyard are both frozen and regressive in that they provide a reservoir of Scottish 'characters', 'attitudes' and 'views' which can be drawn upon to give the '"flavour of Scotland"': a petrified culture with a misty, mythic,

14

and above all, static past'.[8] The extent to which the discourses of Welsh popular television are fixed in a frozen and petrified past can only be established through close examination of Welsh discourses and character types that have appeared in a range of genres. There are undoubtedly certain institutions that have emerged and become synonymous with notions of 'Welshness': rugby, singing, coalmines, the Welsh 'mam', the Welsh chapel, beer drinking; while more mythical, 'Celtic' images – particularly those associated with notions of stoicism and striving in the face of adversity – have characterised much literature and other traditions.

A contrasting paradigm to the Scottish and to a certain extent the Welsh models of national/cultural identity can be found in the Irish soap opera *The Riordans*. Produced autonomously in the Irish Republic and therefore free from the restraining hand of a British/ London-based governing body, the soap made several historic innovations during the 1950s and 1960s. By disengaging the rural family from the cycle of inhibition, authority and conservatism in which it had been traditionally enclosed, it made deep inroads into a dominant ideology which looked to the family – and indeed the family farm – as the basis of Irish society.[9]

The Welsh model, *Pobol y Cwm*, is situated somewhere in between. I believe the soap is becoming increasingly self-conscious, both in its handling of issues socially and culturally specific to Wales, and in its position as a Welsh-language discourse within popular culture. Virtually dormant for fifteen years, the soap has suddenly woken up to the realisation that socio-political references and entertainment are not mutually exclusive.

Textual Forms
The role of character in *Pobol y Cwm* is central to its content, form and construction of a 'Welsh identity'. The characters that make up the 'imagined, constructed' community of Cwmderi all have one thing in common: they speak the Welsh language in various regional dialects. Moreover, they are continually involved in re-creating notions of Welshness which cannot exist in a vacuum but must be defined in relation to another culture.[10] According to one commentator, aspects of Welsh life which have traditionally contrasted with England (besides the language) are *brogarwch* (love of locality), *cyndogaeth* (good neighbourliness), egalitarian social attitudes, strong kinship ties, a tradition of home ownership, scattered and small close-knit communities, a passion for education, mountainous geography, a colonial historical experience, and many more minor

15

details.[11] It is primarily through the characters that these aspects obtain meaning within the narrative.

However, the unity of *Pobol y Cwm* is not created by all the individual characters together but by the community in which they live.[12] Cwmderi, a fictitious village located in the Gwendraeth valley in southwest Wales, is a 'constructed', enclosed community. The social aspects of the Welsh identity can perhaps be summarised by the term *cydymunedaeth* (literally 'co-communityism'): a contrast to the anomic, impersonal, large-scale, techno-bureaucratic society which the rural community stands in opposition to and which is represented to a large extent by Ron Unsworth and his family who 'invade' Cwmderi.[13] 'Welshness' is consequently framed in direct opposition to an English culture/way of life as a series of binary oppositions emerge: rural/urban; personal/impersonal; caring/uncaring. Ron is positioned as the 'outsider' within the community, standing in stark contrast to the locals on a number of levels.

The presence of oppositions brings the text into culturally mythic territory as Ron's synecdochic role embodies this fear of 'otherness' and potential invasion. Moreover, the threat of invasion by the English strikes a historically familiar chord with a nation whose very foundation stems from a self-consciousness born out of challenges and crises involving invading neighbours. Throughout history, the Welsh, who claim to have been the earliest inhabitants of the British Isles, have been continually subjected to attacks from the Irish and the Anglo-Saxons or English. Numerous commentators have thus identified the importance attributed to the creation of myths, ideas and images that have played a significant role down the centuries in giving the Welsh their self-consciousness.[14]

The fictional content of the 'invasion' storyline, therefore, is generated and sustained by culturally familiar sets of oppositions. Moreover, detailed textual analysis of the launch episode of the 'invasion' storyline reveals a series of pair relationships that magnify the cultural 'space' between Ron and the local community and serve as a commentary on the central narrative.

Textual Ideologies

Whilst it is generally recognised that popular genres are not primarily vehicles for the transmission of ideology, the most emotionally saturated entertainment will produce ideas certainly locatable in terms of ideology.[15] The soap encourages viewers to produce meaning in a number of ways and in relation to various discourses. The ideological 'effect' of *Pobol y Cwm* is the extent to which it transmits certain 'ideas' and constructs a specifically Welsh discourse. Issues socially and culturally specific to Wales, such as the sale of second homes to English people, depopulation of rural areas and increasing urbanisation, unemployment, problems facing the agricultural community etc., can be explored through the familial/domestic framework. The personal can then be evacuated of its purely private connotations and inserted instead into a network of economic and communal relations.[16]

Dominant ideology is explored and unpicked within *Pobol y Cwm*, as innovative and refreshing storylines transcend the tried and tested conventions of the genre and cut across many boundaries. One such story focused on the nationally/politically sensitive issue of the sale of Welsh property to the English. This issue has aroused much controversy in political and social circles since the earliest arson attacks on targeted cottages back in the 1970s. The media coverage of the quasi-terrorist Welsh Nationalist group *Meibion Glyndwr* (Sons of Glyndwr) in 1988 and 1989 prompted the production team to introduce a storyline exploring the issues at stake.

The story concerned an elderly, recently widowed character, Gladys, putting her small cottage on the market. Disappointed that several local Welsh people cannot afford the asking price, she is tempted to sell to Ron Unsworth's brother Billy, who would use the cottage as an occasional weekend retreat from Birmingham. However, she begins to receive threatening phone-calls from the Sons of Glyndwr, warning her about selling to the English. After much trauma and deliberation, she is relieved to sell to Meic Pierce, an entrepreneurial local café owner, who persuades her to drop the price. Once the sale is completed, he resells the cottage to Billy Unsworth at the higher price.

One of the ideological strands of this storyline concerns an individual's right to enter the housing market, as buyer or seller, without experiencing harassment or attacks from political pressure groups. However, the 'structures of feeling' of the storyline challenge this simplistic reading. Gladys's position in the narrative represents the moral dilemma felt by Welsh home-owners who want to sell their property at the asking price, but feel guilty about selling to non-Welsh and contributing to the destruction of Welsh communities. Gladys is sympathetic to the nationalist cause and expresses some concern for the preservation of social and cultural institutions. However, encouraged by her brother to get the maximum price, she finds pressure being put on her from familial and political parties. (Significantly, gender differences and the pressures on single women represent another rich ideological strand.)

The existence of a 'dominant' reading of this storyline will ulti-

17

mately be based on the audience's own political/ideological beliefs and the extent to which they sympathise with Gladys's predicament. However, the ironic resolution of the narrative complicates the ideological dimension even further, since it signifies the financial imperative underlying most situations like this and represents to most viewers the most realistic outcome. Furthermore, on a subtextual level, the North Walean origins of the pivotal character in this storyline, Meic Pierce, add another dimension in terms of regional stereotyping and ethnographic myths. (North Walean characters in Welsh popular fiction are frequently stereotyped as being shrewd and money-oriented.)

It would therefore be misleading to assume that *Pobol y Cwm* embodies a single, consistent ideological position in relation to its particular social and cultural identity, since its ideological 'effect' is not something fixed or static but changes and develops as new storylines and characterisations shift ideological sites and discourses into new territories. Ideas and idea systems in *Pobol y Cwm* cannot in any simplistic sense be isolated or perceived as containing any 'commonsense truth' about 'Welshness' or what is understood by the term 'Welsh identity'. 'Welshness' itself is a fluid system and should not be viewed as something vaguely associated with Celtic symbols, Welsh Druids or images of coal-pits and valleys.

Popular Pleasure and Cultural Identity

My research into the role of cultural products in celebrating and redefining notions of nationhood and culture took place through the medium of English in a bilingual comprehensive school in a village in South Wales (some eighteen miles north of Swansea). Despite its bilingual status, the school is Welsh in ethos and is known locally as the 'Welsh School'. My aim was to explore the forms of identification young people have with *Pobol y Cwm* and the extent to which they believe it constructs and contributes to a specific Welsh identity and discourse. I had identified four key areas – representation, narrative, ideology and questions of didactics – and hoped to elicit responses in relation to these concerns. It was my intention not to exclude other issues, rather to encourage an open agenda so that students could identify their own concerns.

The methodology employed consisted of screening the launch episode of the 'invasion' storyline to three groups of approximately eight students. The main structuring determinant was age, with the sample pre-selected by the headmaster of the school. The complexity of my role as 'outsider', researcher, invited guest of the headmaster, female teacher and young adult, cannot be ignored in any analysis of

18

my findings. It is generally accepted that what children disclose does not necessarily correspond in any simple way to what they 'think' – the existence of an 'approved' and what Buckingham has termed a 'distanced or critical' discourse about television must be taken into account and measured against other readings.[17]

Added to this is the risk of unintentionally setting an agenda that is concerned with 'serious', 'teacher-like' concerns, when actual viewing and discourse around a programme may be somewhat different – for instance, singing the theme tune, mocking characters, applying subversive readings etc. The unnatural, public setting for the discussion of an activity normally carried out in the private familial space must also be acknowledged, together with the 'privileged' connotations of the selection process despite its supposed random nature. What the children said or felt able to say was influenced by a range of factors, one of the most significant being my perceived cultural identity.

The students' expectations of the '*Pobol y Cwm* lady', as I was referred to by staff and students alike, would have been influenced by the language I spoke and my perceived cultural/class position as an 'English', middle-class academic. I therefore anticipated a slightly hostile reaction from the pupils, though in reality only sensed it with the upper-school students, who were the most reticent and made some remarks about the subtitled episode I screened. It did, however, emerge in each of the interviews that I could speak Welsh, although the only group this had any impact on was the upper school, who relaxed and 'opened up' once they realised I was Welsh and consequently 'on their side'.

What emerged across all three groups of interviewees was their strong sense of identification with the representations on offer in *Pobol y Cwm*. This social and cultural identification with *Pobol y Cwm* did not extend to urban representations of Wales apparent in the rival Welsh-language soap opera, *Dinas*. In fact all three groups adopted a derisive attitude to this soap, condemning it for its Anglo-American style. Many of the respondents subsequently applied their 'expertise' and superior knowledge of social and cultural institutions when viewing the soap, and were able to measure the realism against their own lived experiences and cultural competences. The respondents' discussion of modality was quite complex and sophisticated because the representations on offer in *Pobol y Cwm* were close to their lived experience of a small rural community. However, when asked if they felt the soap should contain more 'progressive' and less anachronistic representations, they recognised the need for realism and plausibility to be balanced against a remit to entertain and engage the viewer with dramatic/comic storylines. All three groups felt firmly that *Pobol y Cwm* contained positive and realistic representations of Wales and Welsh people. Adjectives such as 'caring', 'respected', 'friendly' and 'humorous' were used to describe characters. The description 'natural' was frequently used. Other aspects of Welshness they felt the soap conveyed included the close-knit community and cultural traditions and values.

The respondents were also quick to identify the social and cultural stereotypes of Wales and the Welsh visible in other genres and discourses. Cultural 'institutions' seen to be synonymous with Wales included coal-mining, chapels, singing, drinking beer, rugby etc., while examples of more offensive stereotypes ranged from the label 'Taffy' to representations of the Welsh as being a bit stupid or backward – for example, the naive and rather stupid police constable who frequently forms a comic double act with his Sergeant, a stereotype which has been used in both *Minder* and *The Bill*, the form of the humour being reminiscent of the Irish paradigm.

The main narrative discussed in each group interview was the 'invasion' storyline, and the characterisation of its protagonist, Ron Unsworth. From the outset, several of the respondents offered a particular understanding of what they perceived to be the 'reasons' for the storyline and the main character's relationship with the locals. In terms of their understanding of the polemical nature of the storyline – the negative effects of English families moving into the close-knit communities – virtually all the respondents supported this dominant reading, in their perception both of the role fulfilled by Ron Unsworth and of the producers' intentions. What emerged was a strong sense of approval of this storyline and of its ability to address a particular social issue and fulfil a consciousness-raising role. Many of the respondents related anecdotes of English families moving into their villages and the harmful effect on national/cultural institutions such as the Welsh language, local chapels etc. Moreover, many respondents felt that the soap should be tackling this issue, thus making itself accountable to its viewers while addressing a 'real', social 'problem'. Older respondents offered an economic analysis of the situation, having gained information from their education, TV documentaries, family discourse etc.

Coupled with this economic analysis emerged a critique of imperialism which in some instances was extremely incisive, revealing an acute historical awareness in relation to a similar perceived loss of language and territory in Scotland and Ireland. Two respondents (one middle, one upper school) made articulate oppositional readings of the storyline, particularly of Ron Unsworth's characterisation, which they felt did not present a fair or accurate portrayal of English people. The fact that Ron functions as an ideological type, a caricature of a 'Brummie', did not really enter the agenda. As far as the majority of respondents were concerned, Ron was not atypical and therefore not anomalous to their lived experiences. This would suggest that their undiscerning view/impression of English people derives from the fact that they had no direct experience of many of the representations and situations on offer on television. As an ideological structure, therefore, the approved reading of the 'effect' of Ron's entry into the community was inextricably linked to the respondents' 'world view' of English social and cultural traditions.

The respondents also felt able to identify what they understood to be a characteristically 'English' view of Wales. Their understanding/ interpretation of 'Welshness', therefore, was frequently defined in terms of what they considered were 'un-Welsh' and typically English traits. Again the focus was on Ron Unsworth. Moreover, they believed that the particular English representation apparent in *Pobol y Cwm* had the effect of embarrassing English people resident in Wales – a position also thought to be held by the producers of the soap. There was little ambiguity, therefore, in the respondents' analysis of the role of the 'invasion' storyline and its invited ideological 'effect'. In defining an albeit stereotypical English identity, they felt that the essence of the representation was a fairly accurate portrayal of what has happened and is happening in Wales.

An underlying imperialist reading of Wales' historical and cultural past was apparent throughout the group interviews. However, the extent of the knowledge, coupled with the nationalist ideological positions being taken up, did surprise me, together with the 'threat' posed by the symbolic character Ron Unsworth. This particular storyline in *Pobol y Cwm* would therefore appear to support a strand of Welsh nationalist ideology that has historically drawn attention to this socio-political 'problem'. The quasi-terrorist organisation *Meibion Glyndwr* have taken on board this cause, and have been active within Wales for some time. What is interesting in this research, however, is the extent to which this ideology has affected and influenced its young viewers and perhaps reinforced positions that have emerged in other areas of their lives – educational, familial, TV etc.

The respondents' understanding of these ideological discourses was clearly framed against what they believed the soap's intentions were in addressing these 'issues'. When asked what they believed the 'purpose' of the storyline was, the response was direct and unswerving in its perception of a critical and didactic purpose for the text.

Oppositional readings of this one-way model were virtually non-existent, with only one young respondent sensing an extremist position being advocated in a discussion of the 'invasion' storyline. His perceived compromised view, however, was immediately seized upon by his peers, who forced him to modify his position and agree with the consensus. This suggests that a text does not have as many readings as it has viewers, but that it invites a limited range of meanings which can be narrowed even further depending on the social make-up of the viewing context.

The programme's remit to entertain without neglecting issues of national/cultural significance served as a constant backdrop to the interviews. Many respondents felt that the soap should receive more publicity, while others believed it should serve as cultural ambassador for Wales now that it had been sold to a French TV company. *Pobol y Cwm* was also hailed as cultural ambassador for South Wales in a discourse that highlighted the linguistic and cultural North/South Wales divide. As well as targeting the home market and, as one respondent expressed it, giving 'the Welsh people a conscience', some respondents felt that the soap should be transmitted on Channel 4 in order to challenge the perceived ignorance of the non-Welsh viewer. This sense of national pride and desire for cultural autonomy and recognition was framed against a resentment of other UK minority cultures who, they felt, had received more positive coverage and discrimination. Suggestions put forward as an attempt to redress the balance included broadcasting *Pobol y Cwm* late at night on BBC2 or Channel 4, or even dubbing the Welsh into English.

Future Considerations
S4C, the Welsh-language channel, has broadcast Welsh programmes scheduled alongside Channel 4 output since its inception in 1982. The effect this 'marriage' has had on channel identity has been criticised by both Welsh- and non-Welsh-speaking viewers and has been described as producing a 'jarring' effect as experimental productions sit rather uncomfortably alongside mainstream Welsh-language soaps and game shows. As S4C's remit does not demand innovation and experimentation, it has catered for the needs of its minority audience by commissioning, producing and broadcasting 'safe' mainstream programming that reflects what is considered to be a balanced TV schedule. Welsh speakers are subsequently addressed as a homogeneous group with 'alternative' programming having little foothold in the schedules.

Now that S4C carries all Welsh-language programming and is seen to be conveniently serving the needs of Welsh speakers, organisations whose remits also include programming for Wales (BBC1/ BBC2 Wales and HTV Wales) have been criticised for their complacency and Anglocentric programming. Consequently, non-Welsh-speaking Welsh viewers have become invisible and are assimilated into the broader UK audience. The problem is likely to be exacerbated following deregulation and increased take-up of cable and satellite television.

In order to compete in a new era of deregulated television and remain relevant to future generations of Welsh speakers, S4C must consider the impact of satellite and cable television on its indigenous programming. It must also address issues of accountability and accessibility and be self-critical and responsive to innovation and shifts in audience demographics. If Wales is not to lose its national and cultural media identity, it must recognise the valuable role that programmes such as *Pobol y Cwm* can play in exploring specific Welsh discourses and a truly national audience.

This essay has attempted to highlight the way certain ideas associated with cultural and national identity are transmitted in a popular generic form, and how this knowledge might be used to explore more general ideas around media representations of small nations and ethnic groups. Clearly there is much scope for more detailed and extensive work to be carried out in this area. *Pobol y Cwm* represents *one* paradigm of popular Welsh-language broadcasting; research into Welsh sitcoms, drama series, youth programmes like *Video 9*, and analysis of regional news output would broaden the investigation and provide a more thorough analysis of how 'Welshness' is produced and consumed in both indigenous and non-Welsh broadcasting.

Notes

1. See for example Wynne Lloyd, 'Soap "sianel" boasting a trio of home-grown productions', *Western Mail*, 22 October 1988.
2. Michelle Ryan, 'Blocking the Channels: TV and Film in Wales', in T. Curtis (ed.), *Wales: The Imagined Nation* (Bridgend: Poetry Wales Press, 1986), p. 187.
3. Ibid.
4. John Caughie, 'Scottish Television: What Would It Look Like?', in Colin McArthur (ed.), *Scotch Reels: Scotland in Film and Television* (London: British Film Institute, 1982), p. 114.
5. In McArthur (ed.), *Scotch Reels*, p. 115.
6. Ibid., p. 116.
7. Ibid.
8. Ibid.

9. Martin McLoone and John McMahon (eds.), *Television and Irish Society: 21 Years of Irish Television* (RTE/IFI, 1984), p. 43.
10. Roger Tanner, 'National Identity and the One-Wales Model', *Planet* 17, April/May 1973, p. 32.
11. Ibid.
12. Ien Ang, *Watching Dallas: Soap Opera and the Melodramatic Experience* (London: Methuen, 1985), p. 29.
13. Tanner, 'National Identity', p. 59.
14. Tony Curtis, 'Introduction', in Curtis (ed.), *Wales: The Imagined Nation*, p. 11.
15. Terry Lovell, *Pictures of Reality: Aesthetics, Politics and Pleasure* (London: British Film Institute, 1983), p. 51.
16. McLoone and McMahon (eds.), *Television and Irish Society*, p. 37.
17. David Buckingham, 'Seeing Through TV: Children Talking About Television', in Janet Willis and Tana Wollen (eds.), *The Neglected Audience* (London: British Film Institute, 1990), p. 89.

Soap Viewing, Gossip and Rumour Amongst Punjabi Youth in Southall

Marie Gillespie

Introduction

The following account is drawn from ethnographic research into young people and television in Southall, a suburb of West London with a population of some 65,000. Its demographic majority is of South Asian origin, predominantly Punjabi Sikhs. Further divisions exist, however, in terms of national, regional, religious and caste heritage. The research examines the ways in which young people use television in negotiating the relations between parental and peer cultures. For young people in Southall who have very little direct experience of white British society, television provides one of the most significant sources of information about, and an important means of enculturation into, the wider society.

My own interest in this area grew out of my experiences as a teacher of English, Sociology and Media Studies in three of Southall's high schools over the last ten years. The present research is based on two years' intensive fieldwork among young people in a variety of contexts – in their families and at school, both inside and outside the classroom, and during their leisure time. Ease of access was facilitated by living in Southall, learning enough Punjabi to conduct everyday conversations, and generally immersing myself in local life during the period of fieldwork. Thus very different types of data, both quantitative and qualitative, have been collected, using a variety of techniques: a survey of 380 local youths; participant and non-participant observation; formal and informal interviews; case-studies and classroom-based data collected while teaching Media Studies and Sociology to 16–18-year-olds. The present account offers a brief summary of the main arguments, shorn of their detailed ethnographic data.[1]

25

The fundamental principle on which the research is based is that an intimate understanding of young people's lives, world views, feelings and aspirations, together with a sense of the social and personal tensions which they experience, is a prerequisite for understanding their uses and interpretations of television. In turn, their talk about television offers valuable insights into their social worlds. The research thus demonstrates how ethnography can deliver media knowledge, and how applied media research can generate the kind of ethnographic knowledge which is usually considered to be the preserve of anthropologists proper.

The essay is divided into three parts. The first part examines the popularity of *Neighbours* among young people and the domestic context of viewing. It proposes that viewing can be an agonistic ritual because parents' and young people's value judgments – in real life, and about screen life – differ. Thus viewing is a playfully combative experience, characterised by both intimacy and censure. It can lead to intimate talk, especially with mothers, and it can also allow young people to challenge parental values. However, it often results in censorious talk on the part of parents as they seek to guide and discipline their children and to exploit the situation for didactic purposes.

The second part takes what I will call an orthodox substantivist approach and examines what young people say about what they watch. Their substantive viewing allows for the negotiation of their everyday lives and aspirations. The central and interrelated concerns of *Neighbours* are family and kinship relations, romance and courtship rituals, and neighbourly relations in the community, which are also the central and immediate concerns in the lives of young people in Southall. They use *Neighbours* to compare and contrast their own social world with the one represented in the soap. The productive tension between perceived similarities and differences enables them to negotiate the relations between parental and peer cultures and to articulate their own emergent systems of norms and values. However, while the substantivist approach is of interest in that it highlights these young people's culturally distinctive engagement with the soap, it is limited and unsurprising in its results. It also fails to explain why young people find talking about soaps so satisfying and attractive; it underplays the sophistication of their competence in the genre and further runs the risk of 'ethnicising' them.

The third part of the essay seeks to solve this problem by adopting a formalist approach, which offers much that the substantivist approach does not. It gets us away from the 'Asian' – 'white' dichotomy and centres instead on a homology between the processes of narration in soaps and the transformation of gossip into local rumour. Gossip, a widespread form of talk in Southall's parental and youth cultures alike – and of course in close-knit communities elsewhere – is turned into rumour through processes which parallel the activities of soap viewers as they construct the interweaving plots of the continuous soap text. A rumour establishes a socially sanctioned version of, or consensus about, 'what actually happened'. The transformation of gossip into rumour is thus a key feature of family, peer and neighbourly engagement in talk. In a similar way, soap talk, which young people associate and even equate with gossip, allows for this transformation into socially agreed rumour. 'What one has seen' is transformed in shared soap talk (gossip) into 'what really happened'.

Young people in Southall see gossip as the framework that sustains the soap opera as a produced and received cultural form. For example, the storylines of soaps are seen to be based on, and communicated through, gossip; the stereotypical 'gossip' character is seen to play a central role in the soap community; and the narrational structures of soap result in gossip among viewers. Soap talk is further fuelled by the gossip networks propagated by the tabloid press, which plays with the double existence of characters in the text and actors in real life. In the case of *Neighbours*, actors like Jason Donovan, Kylie Minogue and Craig McLaughlan are also pop stars, and their star images are amplified by circulation across textual and generic boundaries. Gossip – within the text, generated by the text, and circulated across a variety of related media texts – is integrated into young people's everyday verbal discourse, much of which is also based on this style of talk, to which they refer as gossip.

Thus young people's everyday verbal discourse is informed in significant ways by their soap viewing not simply in its content but also, and more significantly, in its form. This offers an explanation to something which puzzled me for a long time during fieldwork – namely, the way in which young people move so fluidly and unselfconsciously between soap talk and real talk. The two are inextricably linked and, to the outsider, often indistinguishable. The formalist approach offers far more penetrating insights into young people's engagement with *Neighbours*. Furthermore, it is a link which, as I shall demonstrate, is created by young people themselves, rather than a link which is an artefact of the research.

1. The Popularity of *Neighbours*
Soap opera viewing in Southall would appear to be marked more by involvement in the experience than by its extent. In the youth survey

soap operas were reported to be the genre most often viewed with the family after news, comedy and crime. While 54 per cent of respondents (N = 380) reported that they often watch soaps with their families, just under 60 per cent claimed to have done so in the previous week. It is likely that some under-reporting of viewing occurred, since the survey was conducted in the summer (1989), when outdoor activities, especially among boys, take precedence.

Neighbours was the most popular soap among the majority of young people in Southall at the time of the survey, and there is little evidence of a subsequent decline in popularity. In a mini-survey of eighty 16-year-olds, 63 per cent claimed it as their favourite soap, while 54 per cent reported that it was also the soap that most other members of their families watched regularly. My fieldwork would suggest its even greater popularity with the younger age-range, and among girls. The other contemporary soaps received comparatively low scores: *Home and Away* at 18 per cent, *Dallas* with 14 per cent, and *EastEnders* on 6 per cent.

A wide and complex range of factors contributes to the popularity of *Neighbours*, some which are unique to it and others which are common to the genre. The main reasons given for its popularity were as follows: the emphasis on teenage problems, especially with regard to family issues and romantic relationships; the privileging of young people's point of view; the freedom and fun that young people appear to enjoy; their assertiveness and the relative control they exercise over decisions about their lives; the attractiveness and independence of their favourite characters; their humour and way of talking; and the sunny Australian climate and outdoor way of life. However, we need to look beyond what young people say about why they like *Neighbours* if we are to understand their engagement with it and how viewing is incorporated into the rhythms of domestic life.

Viewing *Neighbours* is a daily activity in most households, playing an identifiable role in the scheduling of domestic life. Its transmission-time of 5.35 p.m. has probably contributed to its acquisition of a loyal audience. Activities after school and work are, in many families, strictly gender-bound, with boys participating in activities outside the home while girls tend to remain indoors. Most daughters, especially the older ones, are obliged to do domestic chores upon returning from school: 74 per cent of girls reported that their parents set rules about helping mother, as compared to only 49 per cent of boys (N = 313). The daughter's share of domestic chores is much greater in households where the mother is employed outside the home (40 per cent report that their mothers are employed predominantly in unskilled and semi-skilled jobs; N = 382), when there

28

are more male than female siblings, and where gender roles are prescribed by traditional Punjabi norms, according to which housework is a family duty. Thus many parents have high expectations concerning their daughters' participation in domestic duties, and this constitutes a key source of tension for girls, especially those who have high educational aspirations. Many girls complain about the competing demands placed on them by domestic and school work. Watching *Neighbours* provides a space in the day where they can relax after school and household chores.

Soap viewing serves to organise and regularise domestic time for girls, children and mothers, since they are most likely to be at home at that time. Girls, for their part, tend not to go out after school (47 per cent of girls reported that they did not go out in the evening, as compared with 23 per cent of boys; N = 152). Younger children are more controlled in their movements, especially in street play, since many parents are fearful of the dangers of, among other things, heavy local traffic. Viewing with siblings and mother is by far the most common arrangement. Seventy-six per cent of respondents view their favourite soap with younger brothers and sisters and 34 per cent with older siblings. Thirty per cent view with mother, a practice which is more than three times higher among girls than boys. In contrast, 19 per cent of our sample watch with fathers, and 19 per cent with cousins (N = 80).

It would appear that most mothers condone their children's regular viewing of *Neighbours* because, from their point of view, it is a time structured into the day when they know their children will be, if not always quiet, at least settled down in front of the TV. What might start out as a way of relaxing with their children becomes, for some mothers, regular viewing and an opportunity to communicate with children via the soap.

Some 30 per cent of respondents who usually watch *Neighbours* with their mothers value the way in which the shared experience of viewing can generate a sense of intimacy. In addition, the fact that 45 per cent of girls watch it with their mothers is indicative of the ways in which *Neighbours* draws together the females in a family in a way that other programmes do not. But clearly, intimacy may be heightened by the act of sharing an experience independently of what is shared, although what is shared can become a pretext for intimacy. More girls report this to be the case than boys.

Whether or not the shared experience of *Neighbours* does generate intimacy with mothers will obviously be dependent on other aspects of the family relationship. Given that some mothers understand and speak very little English, it may be the calm or intimate viewing situation, more than the programme itself, which is shared and appreciated. Family relationships are expressed through the types of programmes that certain members of the family watch, or do not watch, together. The formation of family sub-groups around the TV set is not simply contingent upon some notion of individual taste or preference, but is often motivated by the desire to be together.

Some mothers use the situation for didactic purposes, and this is often interpreted as their way of showing their children that they care for and feel protective towards them. It may well be that one aspect of the pleasure of *Neighbours* is precisely the anticipation of intimacy and closeness with mother. It is as though in certain families viewing *Neighbours* becomes a kind of inner sanctum in the family, a private, secure, familiar social space to be shared with younger siblings and mother, but which, at the same time, is not devoid of tensions and contradictions. This is because viewing *Neighbours* is also an agonistic ritual; it may just as easily lead to argument and censure as to intimacy. Viewing with mother also means that translation is often necessary, which some find tedious and difficult. Some girls claim that they find it very difficult to communicate with their mothers, since the latter simply do not understand young people's values. Older boys tend to have more distanced and detached relationships with their mothers, and although they recognise that programmes like *Neighbours* bring some members of the family together, they describe this in terms like 'friendly' rather than 'close'. Soap viewing can also alert parents to some of the traps their children may fall into. Boys tend to emphasise the disciplinary and surveillance uses mothers may sometimes make of the programme, but also point to the fact that soaps can provide role models not only for children but for parents, especially in encouraging open and frank communication within the family.

Some young people complain that their mothers, especially those who understand and speak very little English and who are relatively unfamiliar with soaps like *Neighbours* and the associated conventions of realism, tend to take actions on the screen very literally. This is the cause of many arguments, as are the moral issues which dominate family discussions about soaps. In most families the channel is switched as soon as kissing or any kind of sexual innuendo appears on screen, and it is often the child who quickly grasps the remote control in order to avoid embarrassment or a row.

Parents worry that viewing family disputes in *Neighbours* encourages their children to adopt disrespectful attitudes to their elders, a crucial problem in relation to kinship duty; young people, however, do not regard these arguments as having effects upon their behaviour, but upon their mood. In contrast, they emphasise the therapeutic effects of the mildly cathartic narrative resolutions to be found in soaps. Although many parents feel that their values are undermined by soaps like *Neighbours*, they can exploit the situation to reinforce traditional norms and values, or to renegotiate them with their children. Similarly, their children may affirm, or challenge, parental values around the TV set. Television as an object and as a social experience is embedded in family life and beyond. In using and interpreting soaps, young people are constantly comparing and contrasting their own social worlds with those on screen. At the same time they are extending and transforming their everyday experiences and verbal interactions. Soap talk and real talk are woven together to tell a tale about their lives, a tale to which we now turn.

2. A Substantivist Approach

Talk about substantive viewing allows young people to negotiate 'what is' and what they think 'ought to be' in their own social lives and in the world of the soap. Talking about soaps is important, especially for girls, as it allows them to talk about their own problems, either directly or indirectly, through a particular character or situation. However, in most cases a sense of family loyalty would inhibit most young people from talking about their own family problems – except perhaps with the most intimate of friends – and so often soap talk serves as a veiled discussion of their own, private family tensions. The key emphasis in such talk seems to be on how problems get solved. Young people also see soap talk as a means of bonding their friendships, since in discussing the problems that characters face, they are indirectly giving expression to norms and values through the concrete experience of others, in a situation where most direct or abstract expression would be difficult.

Soap talk is a much more dominant feature of female than of male discourse, and for girls who have little direct or unsupervised access to people outside their kinship and peer networks, soaps are seen as providing an extension to their immediate social experience. While boys will talk among themselves about *Neighbours*, they will tend to talk more about the soap's amusing features than engage in the more problem-solving talk of their female counterparts. In this sense, informants see soap talk as a gender-specific way of communicating and of engaging with the dilemmas facing characters in the soap.

While young people regularly emphasise the *differences* between the soap world and their own cultural experience, in another sense they stress strong *parallels* between the soap world and the social world of Southall, not in relation to content or substance but in terms of the formal characteristics of narration and narrative structure. In certain respects, the soap opera embodies many of the characteristics of local life: the central importance of the family; a density of kin in a small, geographically bounded area; a high degree of face-to-face contact; a knowable community; and a distinctive sense of local identity. Similarly, it is the proximity and contiguity of family, kin, neighbours and friends which generates much of what is distinctive about social life in Southall. While young people's own families and those in their social networks provide their primary frame of reference about family life, soap families not only extend but offer alternative sets of families as reference groups by which young people can compare and contrast, judge and evaluate, and, in certain cases, attempt to critique and transform aspects of their own family life.

Migration and settlement in Britain have meant that Punjabi families are undergoing significant changes in their economic, social and moral environments. Punjabi family life is recognised by young people as being based on sets of norms and values which differ in certain fundamental respects from those they regard as belonging to members of a dominant 'Western' culture. In some families traditional values are maintained, while in others they are undergoing revision. Thus parents and children differ markedly in their relationship to notions of 'conformity'.

In spite of changes taking place in Punjabi families, however, certain fundamental features of kinship organisation prevail, albeit in modified form, in conjunction with particular sets of norms and values. The very high density of kin living in Southall is a distinctive feature of local life. In a survey of over 300 young people, 34 per cent reported more than ten cousins living in or near Southall. Thirty-six per cent of Sikh respondents (N = 194) reported grandparents living in or near Southall. Over one-third of households (N = 365) have between six and eight people eating together. These figures indicate a tendency towards larger households and the existence of three-generational households in just over a third of cases. Furthermore, the very high density of kin ensures that the principles of binding reciprocity, respect and co-operation (rather than self-interest) prevail, even though families are breaking into smaller household units.

Young people's competence in matters of kinship extends to a sophisticated understanding of the central values upon which family life is founded among Punjabi Sikhs. These are encapsulated in the term *izzat* (status, honour and respect) and its opposite, *beizzit* (shame). It is difficult to convey the range of connotations that these

32

terms carry. Embedded within the term *izzat*, for example, is a cluster of religious, moral, social and symbolic meanings: the sanctity of family life is linked to the associated values of family honour, kinship duty, and respect. These safeguard a family's internal, moral integrity; if the sanctity of the family is maintained through the upholding of these values, it will enjoy a good reputation, respect in the community and therefore status and a 'pure' reputation. In Punjabi family life, individual needs or desires are in fact subordinate to the demands of family honour or *izzat*. Many young people find themselves in a position where, at home, parents claim the superiority of Punjabi cultural traditions and family values over English or 'Western' ways. At school or when viewing *Neighbours*, young people claim that individual self-determination and personal 'freedom' is encouraged. While most parents and children are sceptical of the wholesale adoption of Western ways, 'soap talk' is one of the means whereby such issues are negotiated.

In *Neighbours* young people, especially girls, are seen to exercise considerably more freedom and control over their lives than do young people in Southall. Thus one of the most attractive features of *Neighbours* is, for young viewers, watching how screen characters assert themselves, verbally, to their parents and elders. Favourite characters, Bronwyn and Henry for example, are admired because they are good 'backchatters' or because they know how to stand up for themselves and what they believe in. The Robinson family is seen as ideal in the sense that they are loyal and supportive, yet offer their younger members independence, space and privacy. The soap's matriarch and grandmother character, Helen Robinson, also adds to the perceived success of this family's relationships. She is seen as possessing a unique ability to listen to and understand people, including teenagers, and their problems. She is everyone's ideal 'agony aunt'.

Trust between parents and children is a key concern for many girls. Even a slight aberration in behaviour – such as being spotted with a boy in the High Street by a neighbour – may, in some families, incur a breakdown of trust on the part of parents. Open and honest communication may also lead to a breakdown of trust or to parents becoming suspicious that their daughter or son is getting 'spoilt' (in the sense of 'tainted'), and this may lead to even tighter regulation of their child's movements and communications with friends. But some girls claim that they too have reason to lack trust in their parents. They claim that in some cases a violation of parental rules may lead parents to arrange a marriage quickly without involving their daughter in the process of decision-making. Such issues of open, truthful communication and trust between parents and children recur frequently in soap talk and in real talk.

Young Punjabi people in Southall, then, use the fictional families in *Neighbours* to articulate their own emergent norms and values, and to comment indirectly upon their own family life. But while they use white families in *Neighbours* to judge their own, the reverse is also true. Given their limited access to white families, the viewing of soaps provides young people with some kind of insight, albeit fictional, into white family life. The Robinson family household, for example – an extended family consisting of three generations – is seen as sharing certain similarities with Southall families in having kinship links with two other households in the same street. This is, however, as far as the perceived similarity goes. Their sophisticated understanding of kinship ties draws their attention to what most regard as the highly unconventional constitution of most household arrangements, where – either through death, divorce or remarriage – most families in *Neighbours* are in effect 'reconstituted'. Sharing one's house with people other than kin by blood or marriage is considered most unusual. Taking in lodgers, especially those who have lived in the same street, would be considered highly risky, particularly in safeguarding family honour and protecting the family from revelations about their private, internal affairs. Perceptions concerning family life in *Neighbours* may also on occasion lead to a conflation of 'Australian' and 'white' values, and to an over-estimation of the supposed freedom enjoyed by young whites/ Australians.

Teenage romance is central to many of the narrative strands in *Neighbours* and to young people's soap talk, yet it is taboo in the parental culture. Fifty-eight per cent of young people consider that 'dating is normal at my age', while 40 per cent report that 'dating is not normal in my culture and I respect that'. Sixty-seven per cent consider that if young people date 'parents should know about it but be more understanding', while 31 per cent consider that 'going out is all right as long as you keep it a secret'. Only 10 per cent report that their parents think that 'going out is normal at my age' (N = 186).

Dating couples are extremely resourceful in subverting parental strictures. Young people use soap operas like *Neighbours* to work through some of the tensions that arise from their own 'illicit' relationships and from their attempts to keep them hidden from the family. They keenly observe how romantic relationships are conducted on screen, and eagerly follow the ups-and-downs of courtship and its associated rituals. They pay special attention to the language of romance and the conventions associated with declarations of feelings. A successful relationship is equated with the notion of endurance, and this is attributed to skill in sorting out problems, the ability to communicate and compromise, and respect for other people. Observations about the conduct of courting couples and rituals associated with courtship are later included in intimate talk among close friends about their own relationships and their dating peers. Couples on and off-screen are compared and contrasted in terms of their suitability and success.

Neighbours also offers models and opportunities for talking about the tensions which exist between families and their neighbours. The delicate balance between privacy and sociability is a tension which requires working through by neighbours and friends in any local area, but it is a tension which takes on culturally distinctive hues in Southall, where there is a high premium on privacy and where gossip poses a threat. Privacy in such networks is difficult because it is not something that has been valued or even experienced traditionally but, rather, has become an imperative as a result of migration and settlement. If one adds to this the general lack of individual privacy which is a feature of the tendency towards large families often occupying small dwellings, then one can begin to imagine how families encapsulated within close-knit networks cannot escape the informal sanctions of gossip and public opinion.

Gossip and rumour are seen as one of the biggest threats to a young person's freedom and to family honour or *izzat* in Southall. Gossip in the parental culture is seen to be more malicious and harmful than among peers since it usually has more far-reaching and dangerous consequences for young people. It is extremely rare that peer gossip will be revealed to parents, because complicity among youth is high. One of the most consistent condemnations of Southall on the part of Southall youth concerns the persuasiveness of gossip and the instrumental role it plays in the control of social and gender relations.

In most of the relevant literature, gossip and rumour are frequently conflated, and while they do share certain similarities there are important distinctions to be made. Gossip is private information exchanged by a small group of intimate friends. It usually concerns the private traits or conduct of individuals and their violations of social or moral norms. By contrast, a rumour is public knowledge which, as a result of various collective interpretative procedures, constitutes a socially sanctioned version of an event or incident. A rumour is a whole story rather than fragments of information, and as such has much wider currency than gossip.

Academic work on gossip and rumour tends to arise in local

studies, particularly ethnographies. It has been recognised as a characteristic feature of small-town life, where different types of gossip may be categorised.[2] It is important among women in families with close-knit social networks and segregated conjugal roles. Pressures may exist upon women to conform to local standards by participating in gossip networks if they wish to reap the rewards of companionship; gossip serves as one of the chief means by which norms are stated, tested and affirmed.[3] Gossip may be an informal and indirect sanction which is employed where the risks of open or formal attack are too high.[4] Situations of ignorance or uncertainty may produce tensions which result in gossip.[5] Gossip may link up with higher-profile public activity, like public carnivals, to provide a means by which individuals and groups may 'contest territory' in terms of physical and social space.[6]

Rumour fulfils other needs. Rumours may be propagated when individuals pass on stories which enable them to express anxieties that might otherwise remain unacknowledged.[7] 'Fantastic' rumours may be necessary in order to resolve complexities in public feeling that cannot be readily articulated at a more thoughtful level.[8] Certain types of rumour serve as social instruments by which individuals or groups attempt to improve their status.[9] Rumour may be a process of negotiating shared meanings rather than a product of social organisation.[10] Rumour may be distinguished from gossip in terms of their different temporal and spatial patterns and in terms of the numbers of people involved.[11]

In Southall, some young people see gossip as the result of close-knit kinship and social networks. Seventy-four per cent of my respondents agreed that 'Nothing can be kept secret in Southall'; 69 per cent agreed that 'Everybody watches what everybody else is doing'; and 35 per cent agreed that 'Southall is too isolated, it's like an island.' Strongly differentiated from other propositions about the locality, which were endorsed by less than one-third of respondents, these figures support much of the qualitative data in which young people complain bitterly about the closed surveillance they feel themselves subject to in public life in Southall (N = 179).

The intensity of young people's association of soaps with Southall life and with gossip is perhaps most forcefully demonstrated in their reference to the Mrs Mangle character in *Neighbours*. Mrs Mangle is the key 'gossip' character in the soap; she is seen to embody everything that one would despise in a neighbour – she gossips, has no sense of loyalty and, while purporting to uphold the moral values of the community, in fact shows a prurient interest in any aberration in social or moral behaviour. Among young people the term has entered everyday usage as a term of abuse for anyone who gossips – 'She's a right mangle' – even though the character no longer appears in the series. A year after her departure, and her replacement by Hilary as the 'gossip' character, her name still had wide currency. Her character has taken on almost mythic proportions: she is the 'evil eye', the 'maligning mouth'.

The appropriation of the Mangle reference is revealing of the specifically local response to *Neighbours*, where the anxieties of young people are projected on to the Mangle character as the embodiment of the significant threat that gossip poses to their lives. The threat of having a gossip interfere in one's life is most acutely felt by girls, since family honour or *izzat* ultimately depends upon the indisputable chastity of the daughters. One of the primary duties of parents is to marry their daughters respectably, for which a girl's reputation must be impeccable. However, her reputation can be seriously damaged if she is known to have a boyfriend, or, in some cases, if she is merely seen 'hanging around', chatting or flirting with boys in public. The Punjabi marriage system is one of 'wife-givers' rather than 'wife-takers'. The young bride is 'given' to her husband's family and she has rights to dowry wealth. This places very heavy financial pressures, especially on low-income families who wish to marry their daughter respectably, ensuring that she enters her in-laws' home with moral and material 'worth' and preventing dispute. The system places power in the hands of the boy's family rather than the girl's.

This has meant that for centuries in the Punjab unmarried girls have been prohibited or at least restricted from freely associating in public with boys who are not kin by blood or marriage. Settlement in Southall and exposure to British norms associated with courtship and marriage have meant that such prohibitions are not easily maintained. The perceived permissiveness and moral laxity of 'Western' values with regard to gender relations and sexual relationships are felt by many parents to be extremely threatening. In representing modes of behaviour deemed permissive, television, and soaps like *Neighbours*, are also seen as harbouring potential dangers and enticements. But 'transgressions' increasingly occur which place great strain on family life, and in some cases result in a tightening of restrictions. Such stress and strain is further heightened by the difficulties in controlling information about private family matters or about one's children's misdemeanours.

Gossip about such transgressions poses a major threat to families. Gossip thus serves a number of quite significant social functions, essentially those to do with social control. It also helps define status relations, establishes various degrees of closeness and distance among people, and draws boundaries between insiders and outsiders. Although gossip is seen as a gender-specific way of talking, some boys also enjoy it, but girls are seen to be better at it; they take it much further than boys in that it often turns into 'bitching' and spreads much more. According to boys and girls, male talk is only intimate among very close friends and does not spread beyond an immediate, close-knit circle. In one peer-network which I have studied closely, for example, consisting of approximately fifty 16-year-olds, there are six main friendship groupings which are typically segregated along lines of gender, year-group and course of study, except for one which is mixed, containing three dating couples. Within each group there exists a similar pattern: a core intimate group, usually with highest status members, comprising anything from two to four people, and peripheral groupings of two to three members around them.

In several of the groups there is an outsider – often female – who has low status but nevertheless attaches herself to the group. This person, feeling at times outcast and seeking attachment, moves more freely than the others between and across groups. She is generally disliked and seen as a 'stirrer' or a 'spy' because she is in a position to overhear and abuse private information about others. This person is the *chuggli*, or the gossip. She transgresses the boundaries of loyalty in relaying information across groups. In so doing she hopes to acquire (momentary) status by being privy to knowledge that no one else has in a particular group. While she is a useful source of gossip, she is much maligned. Gossip causes trouble between the different groups, vying for status, recognition, admiration and popularity.

Many young people distinguish between gossip and rumour mainly by virtue of the fact that gossip is seen as private talk and rumour as a story for public consumption. A rumour, we might hypothesise, is in fact gossip transformed into a narrative by story-telling processes. These processes involve the social construction and dissemination of a narrative in a specific communication network through a variety of verification procedures. These involve filtering processes which result in the levelling of detail by omission, and, conversely, the sharpening of detail by selective retention. Thus, through a social and cultural process of assimilation, an incident is converted into narrative material for more general transmission.

Rumour is gossip made public. It is less easily confined and controlled since verification procedures have attributed to the story some legitimacy and authority but not an author. Whereas the author of gossip is known, rumour is characterised by authorial anonymity, since it is a social construction. Thus there is a dissociation between the speaker and the message, such that subsequently the speaker cannot be held responsible for the story. A rumour is openly and freely discussed without reservation and without the kind of intensity of confidentiality that accompanies gossip. No trust or loyalty is required on the part of the speaker, who is therefore free to disseminate it more widely.

What starts as gossip leaves information gaps which are later progressively filled through the acquisition of new information and incoming clues that spark off hypotheses which are later confirmed, rejected or held in suspense. Red herrings may be introduced to divert attention. Similarly, time gaps in the acquisition of new information cause delay, and during this period the basic elements of the story may be embellished, exaggerated or distorted depending on the moral or affective investment of those participating in the construction of the rumour. There is a tendency to speculate and elaborate a rumour – especially when faced with scepticism – until it acquires some narrative coherence and plausibility, and to assimilate fragments according to an established narrative theme. Young people often use either previous rumour or soap narratives as models; in Southall, rumours mainly concentrate on stories about girls known or unknown running away from home, about girls dating or marrying a boy of different religion, caste or colour, and about pregnancy and abortion.

Gossip about the transgression of norms poses a major threat to the family, and this explains why the issue of gossip is so prominent in the lives of young people locally and why it is so central, especially for girls, to their engagement with the soap genre. But if gossip is a threat it is also an activity, a way of communicating which is indulged in and enjoyed by many, and which varies from idle, harmless chatter about people to the spreading of scandal and slanderous rumour. Not only are soaps seen to base their storylines on gossip, but the narrative becomes a generator of gossip. This can be explained by specifically textual features of the soap genre, to which we now turn.

3. Soap Narration as Gossip
Narration is the process whereby story material is selected, arranged and represented in order to achieve specific time-bound effects on the perceiver of narratives. A narrative or story is the product of such processes. The distinction between the story that is represented and its actual representation goes back to Aristotle's *Poetics*, but was theorised for the twentieth century by the Russian Formalists

39

through the terms *fabula* and *syuzhet*. According to Formalist theory, the *fabula* (sometimes translated as the 'story') is the imaginary construct we create progressively and retroactively from a pattern of assumptions and inferences based on a variety of perceptual schemata which condition the viewer's reading.[12]

The *fabula/syuzhet* distinction is relevant to our discussion of soaps in a number of ways. First, in focusing our attention on the processes of narration it obliges us to consider – unlike some other theories of narrative – the cognitive and inter-subjective activities of viewers during and after viewing, especially in relation to the verbal discourse that soap generates. Secondly, the processes involved in converting gossip into rumour are closely akin to the viewers' activities, directed at the construction of a coherent story from the fragments of information available. This explains why the teenage viewer's identification with *Neighbours* is more an identification with the processes of narration itself, and with gossip, than with particular characters *per se*. Thirdly, the cognitive processes referred to above, when applied to the continuous narration of the soap genre, find expression in the verbal discourse which young people perceive as a form of storytelling akin to gossip.

Neighbours, like most other soaps, privileges verbal over visual discourse. Low production values and naturalistic camera techniques do not render it visually exciting – unlike, for example, *Dallas*. Low-budget soaps like *Neighbours* bear the marks of their generic origins in radio, where the emphasis on dialogue was seen to be compatible with the housewife pursuing her domestic chores while listening. Thus, apart from a few attractive figures in whom teenagers find some visual pleasure, young people's engagement with *Neighbours* is chiefly via dialogue. Given the proximity, intimacy and intensity of family and neighbourly relations in *Neighbours*, much of the dialogue involves private, intimate talk between family, friends and neighbours, very often about other people, behind their backs. The complex interweaving of different storylines in the continuous narrative depends on a constant succession of revelations about the secret lives of characters past and present, and invites speculation about their futures. For young people in Southall, this way of talking is equated with gossip.

Soaps are also characterised by oral forms of storytelling, defined by specific time-structures which fragment narration across a longer time-frame than is the case in almost any other genre, thus extending suspense and heightening curiosity over days rather than hours. The form is similar to the stories constructed by young people through fragments of gossip which accumulate on a daily basis and often acquire the currency of news or rumour. This relates to one of the most important features of soap narration, the way in which knowledge and information is distributed between the characters in the diegesis and between characters and viewers.

Soap viewers are placed in a paradoxical position, for whereas their motivation to continue viewing is maintained by their curiosity – vital information is withheld during any one episode and in the cliffhanger endings – they are also placed in a privileged position of knowledge which results in their always knowing more than certain of the characters. Viewers, like the recipients of gossip, are in possession of secret knowledge that is shared, and this in turn catalyses further speculation about how a character will react when he or she is also made privy to that information.

What Barthes referred to as the hermeneutic code involves the establishment and resolution of questions and enigmas, and the delicate balance between denying viewers information and revealing it.[13] In soaps, multiple enigmas are initiated, developed and resolved at different rates, and so the viewer's curiosity is in a constant state of arousal. Curiosity is partially appeased by the information to which the viewer has privileged access. As with gossip, we are told the intimate secrets of a character's life, and we know which other characters share this information, but we also know that those wishing to conceal their secrets are unaware that we are privy to this knowledge. This places viewers in a position of power in that they know something others do not, but also in a position of powerlessness in that they are unable to use this knowledge (unlike the case with real-life gossip) to intervene in the course of events.

Much of the activity involved in viewing soaps involves the processing and manipulation of information in a way that differs markedly from the experience of other texts. The continuous narrative means that regular viewers are in possession of a great deal more knowledge about characters and past events than in the case of any other genre – in the case of *Coronation Street* it may stretch back thirty years. Although the broadcast life of *Neighbours* in Britain is just five years (as I write, in 1991), many 16-year-olds may therefore have watched it on a daily basis for nearly a third of their lives. It is not surprising, therefore, that young people learn to live with TV families like the Robinsons, the Bishops and the Mangles almost as extensions of their own lives. The range and depth of background information which viewers accrue over the years in turn facilitates cognitive and verbal activities during and after viewing.

Cognitive activities such as these form the basis of the verbal discourse in which young people engage in both domestic and peer contexts. These are very similar to the processes referred to earlier that gossip must undergo in order to become rumour: the levelling of detail by omission, and the sharpening of detail by selective retention. Moreover, the characters of the soaps are themselves involved in these processes of story construction and story evaluation. The overlapping connections between the large numbers of characters populating the dense social networks of soap offer multiple perspectives to viewers. The cliffhanger endings and the suspense that is generally created through the processes of narration further encourage speculative talk about characters and their relationships. Thus, in making their varied connections between soaps and gossip, young people identify above all with the process of narration itself rather than with any individual character.

Notes

1. For a fuller account, see M. Gillespie, *Television, Ethnicity and Cultural Change: An Ethnographic Study of Punjabi Londoners* (London: Routledge, forthcoming).
2. A. Blumenthal, *Small Town Stuff* (Chicago: Chicago University Press, 1932).
3. E. Bott, *Family and Social Network* (London: Tavistock, 1957).
4. R. Paine, 'What is Gossip About: An Alternative Hypothesis', *Man*, vol. 2, 1967, pp. 278–85; 'Gossip and Transaction', *Man*, vol. 3, 1968, pp. 305–8.
5. E. Evans-Pritchard, *Witchcraft, Oracles and Magic among the Azande* (Oxford: Clarendon Press, 1937).
6. A. Cohen, 'Drama and Politics in the Development of a London Carnival', *Man*, vol. 15, 1980, pp. 65–87; 'A Polyethnic London Carnival as a Contested Cultural Performance', *Ethnic and Racial Studies*, vol. 5, 1982, pp. 23–41.
7. L. Festinger *et al.*, 'A Study of Rumour: Its Origins and Spread', *Human Relations*, vol. 1, 1948, pp. 464–86.
8. P. Lienhardt, 'The Interpretation of Rumour', in J. Beattie *et al.*, *Social Anthropology* (Oxford: Clarendon Press, 1975).
9. S. Smith, 'News and the Dissemination of Fear', in J. Burgess *et al.*, *Geography, the Media and Popular Culture* (London: Croom Helm, 1985).
10. R. Firth, 'Rumour in Primitive Society', *Journal of Abnormal and Social Psychology*, vol. 53, 1956, pp. 122–32.
11. T. Shibutani, *Improvised News: A Sociological Study of Rumour* (Indianapolis: Bobbs-Merrill, 1966).
12. D. Bordwell, *Narration in the Fiction Film* (London: Methuen, 1985), ch. 3, 'The Viewer's Activity', pp. 29–47.
13. R. Barthes, *S/Z* (London: Cape, 1975), especially ch. LXXXIX, 'Voice of Truth', pp. 209–10.

Identity Management and Popular Representational Forms

Breda Luthar

Managing the National Identity

The influence of nationalism in general, and especially today in Eastern and Central Europe, is a result of an erosion of old structures and the reaction to increasing social and economic uncertainty. In such circumstances, the search for a social identity easily turns into the construction of national identity. Nationality becomes a major factor defining the co-ordinates of social identity (in spite of internal social stratification), and it is articulated as cultural nationalism. Political identity is underdeveloped for structural and institutional reasons and appears as political nationalism only with democratic changes. In the case of Scottish cultural nationalism, in Bleicher's opinion, it is necessary to deal with an ideology of anti-modernisation, in contrast to the tendency of classical nationalism – as ideology of modernisation – toward overlapping of culture and power, ethnicity and state.[1] However, for Slovenia, cultural nationalism is both nostalgic and restorative. Also where, in the late 1980s, cultural nationalism has been used politically, it has referred to cultural elements in the search for meaning and for national identity. National nostalgia and romanticism have not only been popularised and commercially maintained, but also produced anew. The main reference point has been differentiation from other nations in a multinational country. National identity has therefore been constituted and confirmed in contradiction to other national identities.

Culturally mediated nationalism is of interest to us mostly as a sphere of culture objectified in texts. It is a conscious formulation and requires interpretation by both cultural producers and recipients, the so-called 'cultural instruments of nationing'.[2] Culture objectified in texts undeniably forms the structure of our memory

43

and identity. We can all remember several canonical texts in our own national literary tradition, as well as films, serials and hit songs which act as mnemonics to a stock of knowledge. The Austrian communication scientist Kurt Luger talks, for instance, about *Heimat* films, song hits, operettas and Austrian sports victories as those media events that contribute to the construction of Austrian national identity.[3]

To what extent is this dominant role of culture objectified in texts – the source of consciousness about unity and particularity – a characteristic need of small nations, or of nations with a weak state-building tradition or which have experienced long-standing foreign domination? It is no coincidence that Australian scholars seem to pay a lot of attention to sights and images of national identity in attempting to differentiate 'Australianness'. Literary, film and television texts, together with architecture, customs and the whole cultivated landscape (for instance, Bondi Beach), represent the objectified culture to which the art historian Aby Warburg assigns 'mnemonical energies'.[4]

A popular text is therefore a piece of objectified culture and at the same time a producer of specific identities. In other words, the content and aesthetic form of a text convey its meaning only through the reception and interpretation which is defined by the common experience of recipients, and objectified in social memory.

Is nationality constituted by *culture* or *will* when nations are formed? To what extent is nationality the result of a system of ideas, symbols, associations and behavioural customs arising from the same existential positions, and to what extent is it the result of mutual recognition and cultural production? For Gellner, neither of these statements is sufficient in itself. Objectivism (culture) and voluntarism (will) cannot be mutually distinguished; nationality is constituted simultaneously as both.[5]

Television is, because of its elaboration of other oral practices of popular culture, especially marked by the 'reinvention of tradition'. The dominant prime-time genres on TV Slovenia, for instance, rework popular folk culture. They are characterised by an anti-modern aesthetic attitude to design, by the use of reproduced artefacts of traditional culture in studio sets, and by a communication code which positions viewers as members of a nation. Nationality is defined by selective use of folk culture, using classic texts and nativism. In this way the cultural nationalism, as Gellner says, 'claims to defend folk culture while in fact it is forging a high culture . . .'[6]

A Common National Habitus

Much reception research within Cultural Studies examines how diverse cultural forms define and position the subject. A central concern has been the identifications they stimulate. We shall try to adapt Bourdieu's basic analytical category of 'habitus' – the phenomenon which produces a system of permanent and transferable dispositions from specific existential conditions.[7] Empirically the 'habitus' can be understood through forms of practice. 'Habitus' is the principle that constitutes and defines forms of practices, including cultural ones – practices of television production, reception and preferences. By extension, a theory of classes (and the connection between class position, cultural consumption and life-style) can also be conceptualised as a theory of national identity/'habitus'.

Lash has equated 'habitus' and the notion of identity with Durkheim's 'collective consciousness'.[8] 'Habitus' understood in this way has two constituent parts: first, the group we define ourselves with (in-group) and the group the identity keeps a distance from (outgroup); and second, classification. Identity, according to this analysis, is in part defined by classification or typification schemes. We constantly classify all objects of material and cultural consumption, for example TV programmes, and at the same time read and evaluate them.

In order to analyse popular television production in terms of the existence of nationally specific life-styles and aesthetic tastes which define television consumption and preferences, it is necessary firstly to examine the existential conditions which define the 'habitus', realised in the cultural practices of ethnicity, and secondly to analyse the maintenance and invention of common identity in variable conditions of existence. We have to deal with the cultural production of a national identity which overrides the different social positions of viewers and unifies them within a common national identity. That is, viewers are positioned within the text as members of a nation.

But to what degree is it possible in stratified societies to speak about a homogeneous national 'habitus', seen to be directing a relatively unified aesthetic attitude? If we presuppose the existence of a national homeland, then this means that the horizontal organisation of the community in a nation transcends any classification which arises from status position (defined through income, education, taste, life-style). Among numerous identities constituting the identity of each individual the national identity becomes at a certain historical moment stronger and more generative than any other. Elwert has addressed nationalism as 'we group-processes' – formed

45

in reaction to the increasing social and economic uncertainty which causes the loss of individual identity.[9]

So, 'Sloveneness', as the 'we-group' reference, transcends this internal class structure. The individual loses the life-space he controls and gains through nationalism, a life-space which is effective if still outside his control. Nationalism erodes the old structures from which the individual once drew his identity. This national identity is, in its articulation and objectification through TV genres, based on defensiveness and nostalgia, but is maintained with the assistance of popular and commercial interests. Cultural nationalism can, as such, easily be instrumentalised for various political interests. It can act as a symbol (which is here to stand for something else) and be filled with a variety of content.

The Intertextual Activities of the Game Show Host

The transformation of the practices of oral folk culture into the TV quiz genre has to be placed within a broader context of cultural practices. These are not necessarily mediated through television. The game show is not something isolated within the universe of other texts and cultural practices, but is positioned within the whole of television as well as within non-televisual cultural practices. Reception of the quiz show *She and He* is defined by the broader television environment as well as the cultural and political context. The concept of the 'supertext' can be used here to express the totality of all texts through which the text of research is articulated. The most defining element of the supertext of this game show might be the additional authorial and political activity of the quiz show host. In recent years a series of secondary texts has intensively renewed and transformed the Slovene tradition of cultural practices – the 'we-group processes'. These have included political pamphlets and literary articles, as well as various TV genres, items in newspapers and even pop songs.

Mito Trefalt, host of *She and He*, has been known for a decade as the organiser of various mass family New Year celebrations (thousands of families in huge market-halls), family sports competitions, social games and family television gymnastics. All these quasi-sports games and group games were not mediated through the media until the appearance of his earlier television show *Wheel of Fortune*. These shows share a combination of elements: sport (family swimming, cycling, running), fun and competition. Mito Trefalt never refers in these programmes to an individual, but always to a family. The popular aesthetics of his performances consist of accommodated folkloristic celebrations based on the ethics of physical and spiritual

46

renunciation and endurance (the way to the winner's title of one of these competitions is usually lengthy and exhausting, since it lasts a whole season); obedience (the leader is recognised as having complete authority over the interaction in the games); patriotism (the competitions are symbolically marked by objects of Slovene cultural tradition); and thriftiness and asceticism (taking part in the show is not considered as leisure time, idling or giving oneself up to pleasures; every participation is 'work being done').

The participants in the television game *She and He* are acquainted with the other activities of the author; participation even implicitly presupposes this knowledge. There is an acceptance of the host's authority as leader. Any enterprise or excess on the part of participants that is not initiated by the leader himself is seen as undesirable. There is consent to the implicit rules of social relations in the broadcast: a particular style of communication, linguistic rules, acceptable and unacceptable jokes, etc. Many have already participated in Trefalt's non-television events and have been admirers for years.

At the time of writing (early 1991) there was public discussion in Slovenia about violence and sex on TV. It was started by Mito Trefalt after the transmission of *Twin Peaks*. The programme, which was broadcast every day at about 11.30 p.m. (very late for Slovenians, who start work as early as 6 a.m.), generated a real enthusiasm, comparable only with the reception of *Peyton Place* or *Long Hot Summer* a quarter of a century before. Trefalt took advantage of his position on the Managing Board of Radio and Television and talked of a preference for locally produced Slovene programmes. He spoke out against violence and sex on television and its negative influence on children and family life. The increasing number of juvenile mothers and abortions, he suggested, was the consequence of presenting sex on television screens. In his public appearance on television – in a verbal duel with the editor of the film programme on national television – Trefalt said that prime-time broadcasting should be devoted to Slovene family programmes which all generations could watch with equal interest and where all the members of the family would have something to discuss.

Hidden behind the concern for the 'mental hygiene of the Slovene family' in this discussion about the national television programme schedules (which increasingly indicate a victory for the influence of aesthetic neo-traditionalists) is the struggle for control over the domestic sphere and its regulation.[10] It is also the struggle for centring social identity around the idea of national particularity and transcending strata differentiation in favour of the unity of 'all Slovenes'.[11]

In this struggle we can witness the confrontation of two political ethics, two different life-styles, and two aesthetic attitudes. On the one hand we have the aesthetics that measure cultural objects according to aesthetic criteria, and on the other we have the 'popular, ethical aesthetics' which evaluate the aesthetic object in terms of life and morality. Form is totally subordinated to function and the aesthetic attitude is defined by common sense. Cultural production thus becomes an important mechanism of social classification.

Ordinary People in the Public Domain

It is possible to discern within the communicative ethos of Slovene game shows more than just the trivialities of a specific style of presentation. There is, in addition, a relationship with authority and tradition. Aesthetic preferences are part of the ethical/political preferences that constitute the life-style of the interpretative community. Tradition is being renewed and restored in response to the characteristics of political struggle and public life. Nowadays it is the 'national' programmes that create a calendar of public events, co-ordinate social life and represent the register of common public life.[12] There are certain kinds of programme – including game shows – which must be viewed as national events and as a part of social reality. This is true not only for their admirers, but also for their opponents. The ways in which a game show adapts the public world of private ordinary person for its audience tells us much about public political life and its constitution through TV.

The host of *She and He* refers, in his introduction, to the participants as well as to the television audience; he permits no objection, no unforeseen excess or reaction which is not initiated by himself. He does not leave the participants time to express joy or disappointment at the end of each game. The result of such an organised use of time in the game show is a complete absence of spontaneous elements. The master of ceremonies has full authority to arbitrate in relation to contested answers and allows no consultation with the expert group or the audience in the studios. He does not allow participants to show initiative in mastering the game. His performance is highly pedagogic and paternalistic, while the audience in the studio and the contestants are passive and subordinate to his authority.

Participants find it difficult to finish their sentences, for they are not used to using a censored and highly formal public language. Trefalt finishes their sentences; he usually corrects them, puts their slang into official literary language and, if necessary, transforms the linguistic structure of the answer. Their slang is thus reformulated into an approved presentational form. In his monologues the leader uses – with a somewhat forced clumsiness – an overly artificial literary language. During the centuries of foreign domination, Slovene cultural nationalism has largely been constituted through its linguistic distinction, first by contrast with the dominating German-speaking nation and later in terms of the evolution of a separate Slavic language. As Bennett reminds us, 'How a nation "thinks" itself is centrally dependent on how it "speaks" itself and on the relation of its language to other languages.'[13] The audience in the studio and the participants – judging from a series of taciturn, nearly pantomime-like performances – are bad at precisely this cultivated literary language. We are thus faced with a particular kind of censorship, since the participants cannot speak their own language – their dialect, their accent.

Conclusion

During the game, the participants become public persons but are denied access to their own language and their own natural behaviour. Their posture, way of walking and sitting, their gestures and facial expressions, the time and space they occupy on the programme, their accent, speech patterns and vocabulary represent a part of their 'habitus' censored by this fictional programme.

Proletarian 'habitus', popular taste and life-style have much in common with the traditional national 'habitus' and conform to the pressure to find a common biography of the nation. Individualism and difference are not prominent characteristics of the proletarian strata. It is only this popularly transformed proletarian national 'habitus' that can occupy the privileged place of fictioning the nation into existence. Even where there is evidence of a persistence of a proletarian 'habitus', its practices are either modified or censored. Folk culture is thus transformed into a high culture of cultural neo-nationalism defined by a neo-conservative political ideology. *She and He* develops a political ethos of obedience, a sense of duty and order. The way in which ordinary people are placed in the public sphere of broadcasting tells us about the nature of public life and political 'habitus' in general. As Paddy Scannell puts it: the world of broadcasting 'is not a reflection, a mirror, of a reality outside and beyond. It is one fundamental, seen but unnoticed, constitutive component of contemporary reality for all.'[14]

Notes

1. Josef Bleicher, 'Die kulturelle Konstruktion sozialer Identität am Beispiel Schottlands', in Hans Haferkamp (ed.), *Sozialsstruktur und Kultur* (Frankfurt-am-Main: Suhrkamp Verlag, 1990).
2. Tony Bennett (ed.), *Popular Fiction: Technology, Ideology, Production, Reading* (London: Routledge, 1990), p. 63.
3. Kurt Luger, 'Habsburg, Heimatfilm and Happyend', *Falter – Wochenzeitschrift für Kultur und Politik*, no. 4, 1991.
4. Aby Warburg, in Jan Assman, Tonio Holscher (eds.), *Kultur und Gedächtnis* (Frankfurt-am-Main: Suhrkamp Verlag, 1989), p. 12.
5. Ernest Gellner, *Nations and Nationalism* (Oxford: Basil Blackwell, 1984).
6. Gellner, ibid., p. 124.
7. Pierre Bourdieu, *Die feinen Unterschiede* (Frankfurt-am-Main: Suhrkamp Verlag, 1984).
8. Scott Lash, *Sociology of Postmodernism* (London: Routledge, 1990).
9. Georg Elwert, 'Nationalismus und Ethnizität', *Kölner Zeitschrift für Soziologie und Sozialpsychologie*, no. 2, 1989, p. 450.
10. David Morley, Roger Silverstone, 'Domestic Communication – Technologies and Meanings', *Media, Culture and Society*, vol. 12, 1990.
11. See Lash, *Sociology of Postmodernism*, p. 25, on the constitutive role of the culture of realism in the formation of English working-class identity.
12. Paddy Scannell, 'Public Service Broadcasting and Modern Public Life', *Media, Culture and Society*, vol. 11, 1989.
13. Bennett, *Popular Fiction*, p. 64.
14. Scannell, 'Public Service Broadcasting and Modern Public Life', p. 152.

Broadcasting Pluralism and the Freedom of Expression in France, Germany and Ireland

Vincent Porter

France, Germany and Ireland are three European states which differ widely in size and political structure. They are all, however, Western European democracies which are members of the Council of Europe and also European Community member states. In all three countries, the national broadcasting systems have undergone extensive re-regulation. At the international level, the regulatory powers of the state have been shaped and limited by decisions taken in the European Court of Human Rights and by the terms of the Convention on Transfrontier Television Broadcasting of the Council of Europe; and at the supranational level by the parallel EC Directive, approved by the EC Council of Ministers. At the national level, state powers to regulate broadcasting have also been limited by the provisions of their domestic constitutions and the manner in which these have been interpreted by their respective constitutional courts.

I will show in this paper that despite certain national constitutional, economic and political differences, markedly similar changes have taken place in the re-regulation of domestic broadcasting. In each country, broadcasting pluralism has been interpreted as economic competition between broadcasters, augmented by statutory requirements for politically balanced programming in news and current affairs programmes. The concept, enshrined in the European Convention on Human Rights, of the citizen's freedom to receive and to impart information, has been replaced by the idea of the broadcasters' freedom to provide audiences for advertisers and programme sponsors, provided that news and information services are politically balanced. In short, in each of these three countries, the interests of advertisers, sponsors and the political parties have taken precedence over the rights of citizens to receive and to impart information. Today, therefore, the editorial freedom of the broad-casters is more tightly constrained than before. On the one hand, it is restricted by economic constraints arising from commercial compe-tition; and on the other, by legislative requirements for political balance.

Pluralism and the Free Market

Two separate philosophies have traditionally been advanced for re-regulating the new broadcasting environment, which has been created by the advent of the new information and communication technologies. They have been termed 'a free market in broadcasting' and 'broadcasting pluralism'. The former approach, particularly espoused by the Federal Communications Commission in the USA and by right-wing politicians in Europe, seeks to establish free market competition between broadcasters, similar to that which exists for newspapers. The latter, mainly espoused by the consti-tutional courts of the Federal Republic of Germany and France, seeks to establish 'broadcasting pluralism'. In practice, however, in no country have the apostles of the free market succeeded in achiev-ing all their aims; while the concept of pluralism, espoused by the courts, remains an ideal rather than a reality.

The vague term 'broadcasting pluralism' covers two separate approaches. One sees 'pluralism' as arising from 'external plura-lism'; that is, the establishment of a number of parallel broadcasting organisations. The other sees 'pluralism' as arising from 'internal pluralism'; that is, the provision of a broad range of programmes and opinions within one or sometimes more broadcasting services. This is ensured by the public accountability, via the state, of editorial policy. External pluralism therefore looks to a number of broadcast-ing organisations to generate ideological pluralism; internal plura-lism, on the other hand, looks to broadcasters to provide ideological pluralism through the range and diversity of their programming content.

For the apostles of deregulation, external pluralism is optimally achieved through minimum, or zero, political regulation by public authorities; and by market regulation in the sale of airtime and subscription payment. Internal pluralism has traditionally been guaranteed by para-state funding, such as the broadcast licence fee, augmented where necessary by the sale of airtime; and by political regulation, optimally at arm's length, of programme diversity and political balance. In recent years, the new communications order emerging in Western Europe has tended to merge these two philo-sophies.

In its decisions, the European Court of Human Rights has allowed states extensive freedom in the economic regulation of commercial broadcasting. In the Federal Republic of Germany (FRG), France and Ireland, right-wing governments have opted to legislate for external pluralism governed by economic regulation, augmented by internal pluralism governed by political regulation. The combination of these two modes of regulation is now threatening the independence of broadcasters. Competition in the sale of airtime makes broadcasters increasingly dependent on the acquisition of rights to popular films, television series and sporting events, whose prices therefore rise accordingly. In addition, political regulation limits the editorial independence of broadcasters and economic regulation reduces the money available for particular strands of programming such as investigative journalism.

The European Regulatory Framework
In Europe, broadcasting regulation is governed at the international level by the provisions of the European Convention on Human Rights, and at the supranational level by the regulations of the European Community. At the national level, it is the decisions of constitutional courts, national legislatures and their domestic broadcasting and competition authorities which shape policy. However, national legislation is limited by the international regulatory framework currently being established by the European Court of Human Rights and, in the member states of the European Community, by the supranational framework put in place by the Council of Ministers and the Commission of the Community.

The ideal of freedom of expression is open to a number of different interpretations; and there is a degree of ambiguity in the manner in which these rights are formulated in the European Convention on Human Rights and in the several national constitutions which specifically regulate them. The concept of the right of free speech is derived from theories which considered that each citizen possessed certain innate political rights as an owner of private property. Thus the right of free speech was derived from the right to own a printing press. However, even today, with the increased availability of broadcasting frequencies, it cannot sensibly be asserted that each individual has the right to own a broadcasting channel. Broadcasting regulation, whether international, supranational or national, has to balance the rights of individuals to receive and impart information against the finite number of channels available.

A crucial difference, which any analysis of broadcasting pluralism has to address, is the relationship between public broadcasting and private broadcasting. Public broadcasting, which is normally wholly or partly funded by the broadcast licence fee, is accountable to the public, via the state authorities; while commercial broadcasting, which is normally funded by the sale of airtime, is primarily accountable to its shareholders. In practice, a pluralist broadcasting policy may interpret the relationships between public and private broadcasters in a number of ways. It is the economic nature of these relationships and their implications for the right of Europe's citizens to *receive* information that are crucial to the re-regulation of broadcasting in Europe.

The European Convention on Human Rights
Article 10(1) of the European Convention on Human Rights provides that:

> Everyone has the right to the freedom of expression. This right shall include the freedom to hold opinions and to *receive* and impart information and ideas without interference by public authority and regardless of frontiers. [emphasis added]

However, the third sentence of Article 10(1) continues:

> This Article shall not prevent states from requiring the licensing of broadcasting, television or cinema enterprises.

In addition, Article 10(2) also allows states to impose a broad range of limitations on the exercise of these freedoms. They

> may be subject to such formalities, conditions, restrictions or penalties as are prescribed by law and are necessary in a democratic society, in the interests of national security, territorial integrity or public safety, for the prevention of disorder or crime, for the protection of health or morals, for the protection of the rights of others, for preventing the disclosure of information received in confidence, or for maintaining the authority and impartiality of the judiciary.

At first sight, therefore, the rights guaranteed to citizens by the first two sentences of Article 10(1) of the Convention appear to be almost completely countermanded by the freedoms to deny those rights which are allowed to states under the third sentence of Article 10(1) and by the provisions of Article 10(2). In recent judgments, however, the European Court has limited, in a number of ways, the exemptions which states may impose on the freedom of expression.

In *Groppera Radio AG and others* v. *Switzerland*, the court noted that the third sentence of Article 10(1) of the Convention, 'in so far as it amounts to an exception set forth in the first and second sentences, is of limited scope.'[2] The purpose of the third sentence of Article 10(1) of the Convention is therefore

> to make it clear that States are permitted to control by a licensing system the way in which broadcasting is organised in their territories, particularly in its technical aspects. It does not, however, provide that licensing measures shall not otherwise be subject to the requirements of paragraph 2, for that would lead to a result contrary to the object and purpose of Article 10 taken as a whole.[3]

The Court has therefore made a clear distinction in its analysis between restrictions which are legitimised by the third sentence of Article 10(1) of the Convention and those which are allowed by the provisions of Article 10(2). Although the former can be used to regulate the arrangements for preventing chaos and interference in the use of broadcasting frequencies, it is the latter which must be used to regulate the content of broadcasts. Any restrictions imposed under Article 10(2) must therefore be both 'prescribed by law' and 'necessary in a democratic society'.

The distinction drawn by the European Court, between state powers derived from the provisions of sentence 3 of Article 10(1) and those derived from Article 10(2), has important implications. The requirements imposed on states by the exceptions allowed under Article 10(2) are more specific than those allowed under Article 10(1). In practice, the European Court now requires states to fulfil two separate criteria to justify any *post facto* censorship of the freedom of expression. First, they must be 'prescribed by law'; and second, they must be 'necessary in a democratic society'. In *Autronic AG* v. *Switzerland*, the Court ruled that although the relevant national law, combined with the international telecommunications law, was probably sufficiently specific to allow the authorities to deny the appellant permission to receive an uncoded television programme from a Soviet telecommunications satellite, these powers were not necessary in a democratic society.[4]

The reception of television programmes, by dish or other aerial, came within the right laid down in Article 10(1) of the Convention, but the third sentence of Article 10(1) did not apply because the Court had already ruled that it does not ... provide that licensing measures shall not otherwise be subject to the requirements of paragraph (2) ... as the Court pointed out in *Groppera Radio AG* v. *Switzerland*.[5]

In reaching its judgment, the Court observed that later developments, such as the signature on 5 May 1989 of the Council of Europe Convention on Transfrontier Television, and the decision by several states to allow reception of uncoded television signals from telecommunication satellites, could also be taken into account. Since the broadcasts concerned were uncoded broadcasts intended for television viewers in the Soviet Union, the ban imposed by the Swiss authorities was unjustified in a democratic society.[6]

So far, however, the European Court has ruled only that state licensing justified under sentence 3 of Article 10(1) is of limited scope. In 1967, the Commission specifically determined state licensing as including 'a public television monopoly as such'.[7] But so far the Court has remained silent on the powers of states in regulating the economic relations between public and private broadcasters, and their implications for the freedom of expression. In *Autronic AG*, however, the Court implicitly endorsed only the technical rationale for state licensing of broadcasting.

Individual Speech and Commercial Speech
In practice, state broadcasting regulation has to balance four separate freedoms. These are the freedom of the individual to impart information and ideas; the commercial freedom to broadcast; the freedom of the individual to receive information and ideas; and the freedom to receive broadcast services. The interpretation of the concept of broadcasting pluralism, as required of national legislatures by constitutional courts, is therefore open to a range of interpretations, each with different implications for programme content.

The European Court has, however, been notably generous in affording to commercial companies the human right of free expression protected under Article 10 of the Convention. One of the defences advanced by the Swiss government in *Autronic AG* was that since Autronic AG was a commercial company, it was not entitled to protection under the European Convention on Human Rights. But in the Court's view neither Autronic AG's legal status as a limited company, nor the fact that its activities were commercial, could deprive it of the protection of Article 10. The Article, the Court ruled, applies to 'everyone' whether natural or legal persons.[8]

In limiting state freedom in these terms, the court has reinterpreted the liberal concept of the bourgeois citizen as the right of commercial speech *plus* the right of the citizen to receive information and ideas. So far the Court has been able to support these twin principles. As yet, it has not been asked to rule on the two related freedoms. These are the right of the individual to express, and the right of the individual to receive, information and ideas which the media *exclude* because they conflict with their commercial aim of maximising profits, or their political duty to conform to the content requirements imposed by domestic law. In no case has the European Court addressed the latent conflict between the right of the individual to free expression – both to impart and to receive ideas and information – and the editorial decisions taken by the commercial broadcasting media. I have argued elsewhere that most of the provisions in the European Convention on Transfrontier Television are so woolly as to be meaningless, that there are few, if any, guarantees for the citizen to receive information.[9] It is therefore only at the national level that these questions can be, and have been, addressed.

The Federal Republic of Germany
In the Federal Republic of Germany, broadcasting is regulated by the *Länder* (regional states), within the framework of the Basic Law. Article 5 paragraph 1 of the Basic Law provides that

1. Everyone shall have the right freely to express and disseminate his opinion by speech, writing and pictures and freely to inform himself from generally accessible sources.
2. Freedom of the press and freedom of reporting by means of broadcasts and films are guaranteed.
3. There shall be no censorship.

Paragraph 2, however, limits these rights 'by the provision of the general laws, the provisions of law for the protection of youth, and by the right to inviolability of personal honour.'

The function of Article 5 of the FRG's Basic Law is to regulate the formation of both individual and public opinion. It is principally inspired by the liberal tradition of freedom of opinion where individuals are seen as defending their rights against the state. But this is mitigated in German constitutional theory by an acknowledged element of social responsibility of the state towards the individual. Consequently, the free formation of opinion is to enable the individual not only to participate in the democratic process of the state but also to find his or her place in civil society and its underlying culture.

This assumes that individuals can freely inform themselves on public affairs and voice their opinions through a public medium. The public medium then takes on some control functions for the social order, protecting not only the state but also the individual. The Federal Constitutional Court expressed this philosophy by defining broadcasting as both 'a medium and a factor' in the process of forming public opinion. The distinction is a valuable one, for it highlights the twin role of broadcasting. On the one hand, the broadcaster is a vehicle for the major corporate and political organisations to shape public opinion. On the other, it can set an agenda and on occasion produce programmes which provide the citizens with an independent source of information on public affairs.

The dual concept of public opinion which emerges from the interaction between individual rights, civil society and the democratic state is mirrored in the provisions of Article 5. Generally, the Basic Law, including this article, is based upon the idea of *subjective* rights, i.e. safeguards for the freedom of the individual, including legal persons. Article 5 forms part of the human rights section of the Basic Law. But the founding fathers also included a notion of *objective* rights, namely safeguards for the democratic state, its institutions and its social order. Article 5 protects the freedoms of broadcasting and the press and gives them the status of democratic institutions.

Prior to 1986, broadcasting in the FRG, which is regulated by the *Länder*, consisted of the duopoly of public broadcasters, ARD and ZDF, financed by both the broadcast licence fee and the sale of airtime. In that year, however, the Federal Constitutional Court sanctioned a new dual broadcasting order. The basic broadcasting service (*Grundversorgung*), which the public broadcasters would continue to provide, would fulfil a standard of balanced pluralism. In addition, however, this could be augmented by additional services provided by private broadcasters, who would only have to meet a minimum standard (*Grundstandard*) of pluralism. The court paid no attention, however, to the economic regulation of broadcasting.[10]

The framework for the economic regulation of broadcasting was established in 1987 by the eleven *Länder* in an inter-*Land* broadcasting treaty. But this treaty adopted a different paradigm for the relations between public and private broadcasters from that used by the Federal Constitutional Court. Whereas the court looked to the public broadcasters to provide the constitutional bedrock of broadcasting in the FRG, the inter-*Land* treaty set out to establish 'conditions of fair co-existence' between them. The treaty established the regulatory framework for the three main sources of broadcasting finance: the licence fee, advertising and sponsorship. It confirmed the traditional licence fee arrangements for the public broadcasters, but it also assigned two per cent of the licence fee to the regulatory authorities, set up by each of the *Länder*, to license private broadcasting. The authorities could then use this money to pay for administrative costs, to subsidise the transmission costs of the private broadcasters or to finance open channels.

Before the treaty, the public broadcasters could set their own advertising limits. Now, advertising on public television is limited to its current average of twenty minutes per day; and no advertisements can be broadcast after 8 p.m. or on Sundays or bank holidays. For each public radio station, advertising is limited to ninety minutes a day, regardless of the manner in which it is distributed across each of its four channels. For private broadcasters, however, the provisions are more generous. Advertisements are only limited to 20 per cent of broadcast time, regardless of the number of hours broadcast – a theoretical maximum of 288 minutes per day. There is no maximum hourly ceiling.

Commercial sponsorship and product placement is generally forbidden for public broadcasters, although sponsorship by cultural, charitable and public interest organisations is permitted. The trend is clearly to rely on the standing practices and self-regulation of the corporations. Sponsored events and foreign sponsored programmes can only be broadcast if they are overwhelmingly in the public interest. For the private broadcasters, however, the sponsorship rules are more generous. Commercial sponsorship is considered to be a legitimate source of programme finance, so long as the programme *content* does not *directly* represent the economic interests of the sponsor or a third party.

The economic arrangements arising from the treaty have already put the public broadcasters in a precarious financial position. The advertising limits mean that the public broadcasters have less flexibility to exploit new technologies or to compensate for cost increase. This is exacerbated by private sector competition for advertising revenue, which has led to loss of income for the ARD stations. Furthermore, increased competition with the private broadcasters for the rights to feature films and sports events has increased programme expenditure; and as a result, the basic service of the public broadcasters has been cut back. It is doubtful whether the licence fee increases necessary to compensate for the shortfall in advertising revenue and increased programme costs will be politically or socially acceptable to the *Minister-Präsidenten* of the *Länder*.

Finally, the *Bundeskartellamt*, the federal authority which regulates economic competition, has decided that competition in the sale of airtime, and exclusivity in the acquisition of programme rights, not programme provision, are the criteria by which it will regulate economic competition in broadcasting. It has therefore challenged a number of activities of the public broadcasters. It tried to forbid a proposal by the broadcasting authority in North Rhine-Westphalia to set up a joint venture between the *Land* public broadcaster, WDR, the multi-media giant Bertelsmann AG and the local newspaper companies to supply programming and advertising material to the new local radio stations in the *Land*. However, this decision was effectively overruled by the Federal Court in its decision to turn down objections to North Rhine-Westphalia's broadcasting law. The Federal Cartel Office also banned a four-year agreement between the two public broadcasters, ARD and ZDF, and the German Sports Federation which granted the broadcasters exclusive rights to screen a number of sporting events, apart from international events and those featuring the most popular sports, such as soccer, golf, horse racing and motor racing. It remained silent, however, when in 1988 the Bertelsmann subsidiary, Ufa Film und Fernseh, acquired the exclusive transmission rights for the German Football League for its satellite channel RTL Plus; and, the following year, the exclusive non-UK European broadcasting rights for the Wimbledon tennis championships.

It is clear, therefore, that in the FRG three different paradigms have been adopted in regulating the relations between public and private broadcasters. The priority given by the Federal Constitutional Court to the public broadcasters, to provide a service of programming based on balanced pluralism, has been undercut by the financial regulations on the licence fee, the sale of airtime and the use of sponsorship spelt out by the CDU-dominated *Minister-Präsidenten* in the 1987 inter-*Land* treaty; and by the competition decisions on the sale of airtime and the acquisition of programme rights, handed down by the Federal Cartel Authority. In addition, the Authority has also constrained the economic freedom of the public broadcasters by limiting their freedom to acquire exclusive programme rights, while ignoring similar activities by the commercial broadcasters. There is therefore a clear regulatory tension between the Federal Constitutional Court – which looks to the public broadcasters to provide the German citizen with a full basic service of programming but which has no economic powers to guarantee them with adequate funding – and the more competitive economic orientation of the *Minister-Präsidenten* of the *Länder* and the Federal Cartel Authority.

France

The powers of the Constitutional Council in France are more limited than those of the Federal Constitutional Court in the FRG. It can only rule on the constitutionality of governmental bills and the organisation of elections to the National Assembly. It met only five times between 1958 and 1971 and on each occasion supported the government. In recent years, however, it has been more active. It is slowly trying to turn the 1789 Declaration of the Rights of Man and the Citizen into a Bill of Rights.[11]

When the Chirac government presented its broadcasting bill to the National Assembly in 1986, the Constitutional Council was asked by several socialist deputies to rule, among other things, on the guarantees for pluralism in radio and in television broadcasting. The government bill proposed to establish regulated competition between public and private broadcasters. Five broadcasters – Antenne 2, FR3, Radio France, and the overseas broadcasters RFO and RFI – were to remain in the public sector. The remainder were to be commercial, including the first television channel TF1, which was to be privatised. However, the Constitutional Council ruled that the restrictions, proposed by the government, on private broadcasting ownership were inadequate.

In reaching this decision, the Constitutional Council concluded that the government's bill infringed Article 11 of the 1789 Declaration of the Rights of Man and the Citizen. The Chirac government had argued that the private corporations would express the rights of free speech of individuals, and that therefore they needed minimal political regulation. Economic regulation by the market would suffice. For the Constitutional Council, however, the guarantee of socio-cultural pluralism in broadcasting had to take priority over the right to own a radio or television station. It ruled that

> the listeners and viewers, who are the majority of the essential beneficiaries of the liberty proclaimed in Article 11 of the *Déclaration* of 1789, [must be] able to exercise their free choice without being prevented by private interests or by the state, or becoming objects in a market.[12]

This decision made the preservation and development of socio-cultural pluralism the prime task for the new broadcasting law; and for the new body for broadcasting regulation, the Commission Nationale de la Communication et des Libertés (CNCL), and its successor body, the Conseil Supérieur de l'Audiovisuel (CSA). The government met the criticisms of the Constitutional Council by increased external pluralism. It tightened the media ownership rules. Its original proposals for limiting broadcasting ownership to a 25 per cent national share were replaced by more detailed provisions. The new regulations limited the cumulative ownership of shares in different broadcasting sectors; and complemented these by additional checks designed to prevent multi-media concentration. The original proposal limiting foreign ownership of broadcasting stations to 20 per cent, except for satellite broadcasting, was preserved.

During its passage, the government bill was amended by the Senate to delegate to the CNCL the economic regulation of the sale of airtime, for both public and private broadcasters. By the end of the following year, the CNCL had decreed that the commercial television channels, La Cinq and M6, could sell an annual average of up to six minutes per hour of advertising, with no more than nine minutes in any one hour. However, the most popular channel, TF1, could sell up to twelve minutes in any one hour. The two public television channels, Antenne 2 and FR3, which are not allowed to interrupt their programmes with advertising, could sell an annual average of up to nine minutes per hour of advertising time, with a maximum of fifteen minutes in any one hour.[13] However, the government retained for itself regulations concerning sponsorship, the level of the licence fee, and the broadcasting of cinema films.

Under the 1986 Broadcasting Act, therefore, three commercial television channels – TF1, La Cinq and M6 – competed in the sale of airtime with the two public channels, A2 and FR3, which were also supported by the licence fee. A sixth channel, Canal Plus, which broadcasts encrypted signals, is mainly financed by subscription but does carry a little advertising.

The expansion in the French television market has proved impossible to sustain. In 1986, the Chirac government cut the licence fee. TF1 now effectively monopolises the advertising market, carrying more advertisements than are justified by its audience share. While TF1 has proved a commercial success, La Cinq and M6 have both lost money (La Cinq ceased operations in April 1992); and A2 and FR3 have now been merged under a single Director-General. The programming on most channels is very similar, and in this new competitive environment many French viewers have turned to the subscription channel, Canal Plus, for different, and often better, programmes.

In commercial terms, then, the two winners are the commercial channel TF1 and the subscription channel Canal Plus. The two public channels, Antenne 2 and FR3, are currently facing an uphill fight in the battle for audiences, and will schedule complementary programming. The message of the market-place is clear. Economic regulation in France has been mismanaged: there is insufficient advertising revenue to support five television channels. The problem is that French politicians want to have their television programmes provided 'for free' by the advertisers. The licence fee has not kept pace with increased costs, but Canal Plus has been successful because it has found a new source of broadcasting finance.

Ireland

In the Republic of Ireland, the broadcasting environment is significantly different from that of France and Germany, but even so, the same general pattern can be observed. As a small country with a population of only some 3.5 million, Ireland has a small economic base to fund its broadcasting activities. In addition, in the north and east of the country many of the population can receive signals from British television. However, because of the mountain range in the middle of the country, citizens in the south and west can only receive television signals from the public broadcaster, RTE, thus intensifying the social divisions in the country.

The original role of RTE was to establish a distinctive informational and cultural environment for Ireland, and to prevent colonisation by British broadcasting. Until the mid-1960s, most politicians, especially those in Fianna Fail, which traditionally dominated Irish broadcasting policy, opposed foreign broadcasting as a form of cultural imperialism. But a decade later, attitudes had changed and the coalition government wanted to modernise Ireland's predominantly rural economy by recognising that one of the main functions of broadcasting could be to open windows rather than to close them. For this reason, the government was happy to see the growth in urban areas of cable systems relaying British television programmes. The public broadcaster, RTE, diversified into cable by taking over the major private cable operators, including Dublin's largest cable network, divested to Irish Telecom in 1991. For most purposes, therefore, Ireland was effectively divided into urban multi-channel and rural single channel areas.

But the economic expansion of RTE raised other problems for Irish politicians, especially the country's dominant political party, Fianna Fail, which had traditionally regarded RTE as one of its fiefdoms. By 1970, RTE relied on advertising for half its revenue. In order to meet competition from British broadcasters in its most populous areas, RTE increasingly had to rely on imported entertainment programmes and concentrated its production efforts on news and current affairs programmes. Increased competition also meant that news, and particularly current affairs programmes, had to become more audience-oriented. No longer could Irish politicians rely on the public broadcasters to give them an electronic soapbox for their views. In particular, the decline in deference among broadcasting journalists was resented by Charles Haughey, then leader of Fianna Fail. The RTE journalists were accused by Fianna Fail of denying the party an outright victory in the 1987 General Election by their coverage of the recent cuts in health spending. Worse, during a radio interview an RTE journalist accused the Minister of Transport and Tourism of corruption.

Despite appointing an RTE Authority dominated by Fianna Fail supporters, it was no longer possible for the government to impose direct political censorship over RTE's news and current affairs programmes. In addition, it had an economic rationale. Like many other West European governments, it set aside its traditional belief in Keynesian economic policies and replaced them with the new-liberal orthodoxy. Commercial broadcasting offered new opportunities for capital investment. In future it would be competition and the free market which would shape the broadcasting economy. Consumer choice would therefore cut back the excessive political influence of the public broadcaster.

The Fianna Fail government therefore decided to end RTE's monopoly over the coverage of national politics by licensing new national commercial radio and television stations. In this manner, it was argued, it could create alternative sources of news and current affairs programmes outside the control of RTE.[14] To achieve this goal, the Minister didn't just create licences for local commercial stations, as the previous coalition government had proposed, but, ignoring the advice of his officials, decided to award franchises for national radio and television stations. For Fianna Fail the political goal of establishing a national news and current affairs service outside RTE was more important than recognising the economic constraints on commercial broadcasting.

Although some local radio stations were commercially viable since they could offer their listeners an alternative programming service, one of them, Radio West Galway, had to be taken over by a Dublin station after going bankrupt. Worse, the national commercial radio station, Century, which was set up under the 1988 Broadcasting Act, was unable to compete with RTE's pop radio channel, 2FM. In the capital city, Dublin, Century lagged behind not only the RTE stations but also the local stations, Capital and 98FM. Faced with financial disaster, Century's owners blamed RTE, claiming that their low advertising revenue was caused by RTE's predatory pricing. This view was rejected, not only by RTE's management but also by the advertisers.[15]

In order to save his over-ambitious plans for broadcasting, the Minister of Communications took powers in the 1990 Broadcasting Act to cut RTE's revenues. Initially he proposed to give one-fifth of the licence fee revenue to the IRTC, the regulatory authority for commercial broadcasting, to disperse to the national and local commercial stations; and to require RTE to change 2FM from a pop station to an education and farming channel. He backed off, however, in face of the political furore his proposals created. Instead, he took powers to restrict RTE's advertising revenue. Only 7.5 per cent of RTE's total broadcasting time on radio and television could be used for advertising, and there could be no more than five minutes of commercials in any one hour. In addition, it was to be RTE's responsibility to ensure that its advertising income did not exceed its licence fee revenue. To ensure compliance, any excess income would be deducted from RTE's budget for the following year.[16]

According to the Minister, the 7.5 per cent limit on RTE's advertising time would divert around £12 million from RTE to the commercial broadcasting sector and to the newspaper industry. In his view, they needed the increased revenue to survive the strong competition from RTE. His 7.5 per cent limit on RTE's advertising time was derived from the 15 per cent limit imposed in the EC Broadcasting Directive. Since half of RTE's revenue would come from the licence fee, it was only allowed half the advertising time allotted to commercial stations. The tougher restrictions on RTE advertising income were justified by the duty to ensure political pluralism imposed by the EC Directive. For the Minister, the diversity of opinions within the electronic media could only be ensured by external pluralism between competing radio and television stations. In particular, he had a duty to ensure that there were sources of radio and television news outside the control of RTE. This was why RTE's dominance over the Irish advertising market had to be eliminated. 'The whole principle behind this legislation is the need for pluralism of information of the media generally and of entertainment within this country coming from Irish sources.'[17]

Ironically, it is unlikely that the government's measures will achieve the desired effect. The advertising industry considers that the financial difficulties of the commercial stations were caused by the limited size of the Irish economy. Furthermore, by capping RTE, the Minister would engineer a large increase in the price of airtime on RTE, especially in the slots adjacent to popular programmes. This could well improve RTE's competitive position in the advertising market rather than worsen it. In addition, RTE can give 'free advertising' to loyal advertisers, once it has filled its quota. And since there was no guarantee that the new broadcasters would be able to deliver large audiences, it was highly likely that the principal beneficiary from any switch in Irish advertising spending would be Ulster Television, the British-licensed commercial television company broadcasting from Northern Ireland. This can already reach half the Irish population and would probably increase this percentage using the new cable and MMDS networks.

The attempt to increase external pluralism in Irish broadcasting, by shackling RTE in order to facilitate the growth of TV3 and Century, may well result in the increased dominance of a British-licensed television station which broadcasts to all of Northern and most of Southern Ireland. Not surprisingly, the traditional view is re-emerging that the prime role of Irish broadcasting policy is to defend national culture from British cultural imperialism. Politicians and advertisers now recognise that RTE cannot compete successfully against British and satellite stations if it is inadequately funded.

It is clear, therefore, that in all three countries – the FRG, France and Ireland – the institutions by national governments of increased external pluralism in their domestic broadcasting has introduced varying degrees of financial instability into their broadcasting systems. In each country, the domestic broadcasters have had to compete for a limited pot of domestic advertising revenue. In the wealthiest of the three countries, the FRG, the principal private broadcaster, RTL Plus, has moved into profit, but economic competition has forced the public broadcasters to cut back their basic service. In France, competition has brought economic instability into the broadcasting market; and in Ireland, the smallest of the three countries, there is the threat that foreign broadcasters will benefit at the expense of those licensed domestically.

Internal Pluralism
The increased economic regulation of broadcasting in all three countries has also been accompanied by expanded political regulation of programme content. In the FRG, the 1987 Inter-*Land* Broadcasting Treaty interpreted the requirement of the Federal Constitutional Court that all private broadcasters should meet a minimum standard of pluralism by requiring each broadcaster to

> essentially represent the plurality of opinions. Full-time general channels must give appropriate expression to the significant

political, ideological and social forces and groups; minority views are to be taken into account. The potential to offer ... specialist channels shall remain unaffected by those provisions.[18]

The rule is important since, when they were awarding licences, all the *Länder* gave priority to full-time general interest channels of mixed programming. The approach is essentially derived from the responsibilities of public service broadcasters. Full internal pluralism in the private sector is not an absolute requirement, but full external pluralism is deemed by law not to exist until there are at least three private national channels.

In France, all broadcasters are required by the CSA, which replaced the CNCL, to guarantee honesty and informational pluralism in their programmes. The specific administrative measure used by the CSA to regulate pluralism is the rule of three thirds. First introduced by President Pompidou's Prime Minister, Chaban-Delmas, the rule requires all broadcasters to give equal airtime to the government, to politicians affiliated to the majority party in the National Assembly, and to politicians affiliated to the minority parties. Although this rule has become increasingly difficult to implement in practice as splits and divisions occur in French politics, the CSA still carefully times the appearance of political spokespersons on French television.

In Ireland, the 1988 Radio and Television Act requires all commercial stations to devote not less than 20 per cent of broadcasting time to news coverage, including not less than two hours of news and current affairs between 7 a.m. and 7 p.m. Furthermore, each station has to ensure that the news is presented 'in an objective and impartial manner'; and the IRTC had to draw up a code of practice which regulated the availability of party political broadcasts and ensured balanced coverage of elections.

As well as these administrative controls over broadcasting, Irish governments have also retained the right of direct political censorship. Particularly contentious has been the ban imposed in the early 1970s by the Fianna Fail government, under section 31 of the 1960 Broadcasting Authority Act, to forbid the appearance on RTE programmes of anyone advocating political violence. The then government sacked the entire membership of the RTE authority when they supported the protest of the RTE's management and staff against this act of state censorship. However, when the Fine Gael/Labour opposition was returned to power, it kept the ban. It merely introduced the 1976 Broadcasting Authority (Amendment) Act, which required approval by the Dáil for the banning from the airwaves of specific groups. From 1976, the Minister of Posts and Telegraphs has issued annual orders banning from the airwaves, but not from the press, expressions of the views of the Provisional IRA and other named groups. This ban, together with the parallel ban imposed by the UK Home Office in 1988, has been appealed to the European Court of Human Rights.

In 1982, the Irish Minister of Posts and Telegraphs also banned RTE from transmitting any party political broadcasts for the general elections by Sinn Féin, the legal political party of the Provisional IRA. Sinn Féin challenged the constitutionality of this directive under Article 40.6.1 of the 1937 constitution, which guarantees free speech. The Irish Supreme Court reiterated the government's view that the defence of republican democracy was more important than the individual's right of free speech. 'A democratic state has a clear and bounden duty to protect its citizens and its institutions from those who seek to replace law and order by force and anarchy.'[19]

Conclusion
It is clear that all three countries under review have implemented both external and internal pluralism in the re-regulation of their broadcasting systems. The advent of external pluralism has introduced increased competition – a form of economic regulation for broadcasting which has destabilised the market for both programme production and the acquisition of programme rights, leaving broadcasters with proportionately less funds to finance production of their own news and current affairs programmes.

The powers which states have assumed to implement external pluralism clearly have informational implications for the rights of citizens, under Article 10 of the European Convention on Human Rights, but as yet no state has been challenged in the European Court of Human Rights and therefore the Court has not handed down any specific ruling on this issue. However, the principal stance taken by the Court, which is likely to affect any future ruling, is that Article 10 of the Convention affords protection to both individual speech and commercial speech. It is therefore unlikely to deny free speech to any broadcasting organisation licensed by a state, unless it is covered by the provisions of Article 10(2) of the Convention. By adopting this stance, the Court has *reinterpreted* the right of citizens to receive information and ideas, guaranteed in Article 10 of the Convention, to mean only information and ideas deemed not to conflict with the economic interests of the broadcasters, or with the requirements for political balance imposed by the several national regulatory authorities. The right to impart information and ideas has been similarly reinterpreted. In practice, therefore, the right to free expression in broadcasting for individuals has been ceded by the Court to individual states to allocate, as they wish, to the separate corporations which they choose to license, whether public or private.

The powers of states to insist on the internal pluralism of broadcasts, combined with the increased competition in the broadcasting markets and the aim of all commercial broadcasters to generate maximum profits for their shareholders, mean that the broadcasters will have fewer funds for their own news and current affairs programmes. They will therefore increasingly have to act as megaphones for the voices of politicians. In France and Ireland, where respectively the Gaullist and Fianna Fail parties traditionally looked to ORTF and to RTE to be their governmental megaphones, the new pluralism has spread the access to airtime more widely across all the main political parties, and to 'experts' of all political persuasions. In the FRG, where the decentralisation of broadcasting among the *Länder* always meant that political power was broadly spread, increased economic competition has led to tighter budgets for the public broadcasters and to shorter, more upbeat news broadcasts from their private competitors.

In the FRG, the Federal Constitutional Court saw broadcasting both as a medium of communication and as a factor of communication. By this it drew a distinction between the responsibility of broadcasters to transmit the views of others – such as the political parties or the churches – and their duty to contribute to public debate, not merely by setting the broadcasting agenda, but also by initiating their own investigations and inquiries into matters of public interest. The new regulatory arrangements for broadcasting which are being established are likely to decrease the role which broadcasting can play as a *factor* in communication policy, but to increase its role as a *medium for communication*, whether for advertisers, film producers, sports promoters, public relations organisations or politicians. Slowly, but inexorably, broadcasting is being brought under the control of free market forces and the main political parties.

The author would like to acknowledge the assistance of his colleagues Richard Barbrook and Suzanne Hasselbach in the research for this paper; and the Economic and Social Research Council for its partial financial support.

Notes

1. For a more extensive review see Vincent Porter, 'The Re-regulation of Television: Pluralism, Constitutionality and the Free Market in the USA, West Germany, France, and the UK', *Media, Culture and Society*, vol. 11 no. 1, 1989.
2. European Court of Human Rights, *Groppera AG and others* v. *Switzerland*, 12 *European Human Rights Reports*, 1990, p. 339.
3. Ibid.
4. European Court of Human Rights, *Autronic AG* v. *Switzerland*, 12 *European Human Rights Reports*, 1990, pp. 503–4.
5. Ibid., p. 500.
6. Ibid., p. 503.
7. European Commission of Human Rights, *Yearbook XI* (Strasbourg: Council of Europe, 1967), p. 464.
8. *Autronic AG*, *European Human Rights Reports*, p. 499.
9. See Vincent Porter, 'Broadcasting Re-regulation in Europe – Citizenship and Consumerism', *EBU Review (Programmes, Administration, Law*, 1990), vol. XLI no. 6, pp. 21–5.
10. For a detailed analysis see S. Hasselbach and V. Porter, 'The Re-regulation of West German Broadcasting – recent decisions of the Federal Constitutional Court', *Politics and Society in Germany, Austria and Switzerland*, vol. 1 no. 2, Winter 1988.
11. Cf. J. Keeler and A. Stone, 'Juridical-Political Confrontation in Mitterand's France', in G. Rossi, S. Hoffman and S. Malzacher (eds.), *The Mitterand Experiment* (Cambridge: Polity Press, 1987).
12. France: Constitutional Council, Decision no. 86–217 DC du 18 Septembre 1986 Loi Rélative à la Liberté de Communication, *Journal Officiel de la République Française*, 19 Septembre, 11295.
13. Commission Nationale de la Communication et des Libertés, *Rapport Annuel: Novembre 1986–Novembre 1987*, Paris, 1987.
14. Ray Burke, Speech in Dáil Éireann, *Parliamentary Debates*, 7 June 1990: 1569–1585.
15. See Colum Kenny, 'Levelling the Playing Pitch', *Playback*, April 1990, and 'RTE in "Submarine War" says TV3 Chairman', *Playback*, December 1989.
16. Irish Republic, *The Broadcasting Act 1990* (Dublin: The Stationery Office, 1990).
17. Ray Burke, 'Why RTE Must be Tuned in for the 1990s', *Irish Independent*, 22 June 1990, p. 10.
18. Federal Republic of Germany, Inter-*Land* Treaty, *Staatsvertrag zur Neuordnung des Rundfunkwesens in der Bundesrepublik Deutschland*, 1/3 April 1987, in *DLM Jahrbuch 88*, pp. 307–15.
19. Irish Supreme Court, *The State (at the Prosecution of Sean Lynch)* v. *Patrick Cooney and the Attorney General*, [1982] *Irish Reports*, p. 367.

Pan-European Television News: Towards A European Political Public Sphere?

Stig Hjarvard

Introduction

As a response to the changes in the media landscape during the last decade, media research has taken up again some central questions from its youth. Early media research's preoccupation with the relation between the mass media and the democratic structures and processes of society has been revisited in the light of deregulation and the internationalisation of the media. The role of electronic media in sustaining and structuring a public space for representation and exchange of cultural and political information and values has again been placed at the top of the research agenda. The role of radio and television in the construction of such a space has been the subject of both empirical and theoretical investigation in recent years, and in particular the existing Western European institutional structure, the public service model, has been examined.

The first part of this essay analyses European TV news projects in a historical context, from the early considerations of a 'European Newsreel' during the establishment of Eurovision in the 1950s to the attempts to use satellite technology during the 1980s, with the 'Euronews' project as the latest example. The analysis focuses on the public service broadcasters' attempts to provide an alternative pan-European news service to the commercial competitors CNN and Sky News. This part of the analysis is based on study of the archives of the European Broadcasting Union. Secondly, a pan-European news service is considered theoretically as a part of a European political public sphere. Applying Jürgen Habermas's analysis of the structural transformation of the public sphere to television, it is pointed out that the original (bourgeois) conception of the public sphere differs from the notion as it is understood in the underlying assump-

71

tions of national public service broadcasting. It is further argued that Habermas's theory, as well as the public service concept, cannot be applied to a European political public sphere without major modifications. I discuss how the national and European public spheres differ from each other in terms of institutional structure and social/class basis. A consideration of these differences is vital for a pan-European public service news channel.

Before analysing the development of pan-European television news, I will specify some basic features of the present situation of television in Europe. First, we should address the fact that the old Western European public service broadcasting institutions have reached a crisis. It is not only an economic and political crisis following from increased competition from the commercial newcomers, but also a broader social crisis, which can be characterised as a *crisis of representation*. The representation of a *national* public space has become an increasingly difficult task, and the idea of a common national culture is under heavy attack. The breaking up of monopoly situations and increased competition have laid bare a much more complex cultural landscape, with different cultures crossing both national and social borders and contesting existing public service assumptions about good and bad taste. Public service broadcasting has played a key role in the construction of a national cultural and political unity,[1] but as a result of the disintegration of the national community in general, and the erosion of the national state's authority in particular, it is becoming even more difficult to exercise this function.

The crisis of representation is rooted in a *loss of authority*. As Williams has argued, social developments have made the size of the nation state inadequate: 'It is at once too large and too small for the range of real social purposes.'[2] The tasks of the nation state are increasingly carried out on a regional and especially a transnational level. The nation state is out of step with the internationalisation (and regionalisation) of capital. Furthermore, extensive immigration from Third World countries and the periphery of Europe has created a multilingual and multi-ethnic population in the urban centres of many of the former European colonial powers. The authority of the nation state, and with it the national culture and the national political sphere, is no longer indisputable.

Policies of deregulation and an underlying neo-conservative philosophy have contested the validity of public regulation of the media. According to neo-conservative philosophy, the market provides a better guarantee of diversity and public satisfaction. Within this philosophy, public service is synonymous with a paternalistic attitude and is considered outdated as a cultural institution. And the deregulation process did in fact reveal that the public service structure rested on political and cultural constraint: when people were allowed to choose, they actually chose something new. The loss of authority was twofold. On the one hand, the very legitimacy of public regulation was being contested by the ruling neo-conservative parties. On the other hand, the state itself and its parliamentary institutions were losing authority. The problem of representation became acute: for whom, in what social space and for what purpose should the public service broadcasters provide symbolic representation?

Developments in the 1980s have demonstrated that the commercial media are not capable of providing a satisfactory alternative to the public service broadcasters. Although the break-up of the monopoly initially resulted in an increase of available choices and a proliferation of new (commercial) means of expression, subsequent developments have shown a clear tendency towards institutional concentration and a standardisation of media content and form. Deregulation of the broadcasting sector and the communication sector in general seems in the long term to limit the broadness and variation of the supply of political communication and information that is publicly available. At the same time the supply of special information services on, for instance, financial, technological and legal matters increases, but something as simple as the pricing policy of these services makes them in practice inaccessible to the larger population. The combination of deregulation and the information revolution is likely to widen rather than reduce the information gap.

The prospect of such a limitation of the public political culture has resulted in a re-evaluation of the public service concept. Media researchers who in the past have severely criticised the practice of the national public service institutions now argue for a renewal of the public service concept and a political effort to defend and develop broadcasting based on public service principles. There is disagreement, however, about to what extent it is necessary to break with the old practices of the public service tradition.

It is both inevitable and desirable that a public political and cultural space is developed on an international/transnational level, and broadcasting has once again a key role to play in this process. At the end of a well-known study of the media and the public sphere, Garnham points out the necessity of establishing institutional structures on an international level to secure public regulation and control of the audiovisual representation of an international public sphere.

These structures are necessary, if political development is to keep pace with economic development:

> ... the current process by which national media control is being eroded is part of that process by which power is being transferred in the economy to the international level without the parallel development of adequate political or communication structures. [...]
>   Not only do we face the challenge of sustaining and developing the public sphere at a national level. Such a development will simply be bypassed if we do not at the same time and perhaps with greater urgency begin to develop a public sphere where at present one hardly exists at the international level.[3]

This objective, which I share, raises a number of both concrete and political-philosophical questions. What type of public sphere should the broadcasting institutions represent at the international level? If the international public sphere is to be understood as a *European* public sphere, then how is this European dimension to be defined and demarcated? What European and national political institutions should the political public sphere be related to? Which kind of institutional framework should have the authority to exercise the representation of a European public space?

Two Traditional Assumptions

In the numerous analyses and discussions of the new television situation in (Western) Europe two assumptions are generally taken for granted. To begin with, it is assumed that the historical development of television can be described as a transformation from a national to an international context. Television is seen as initially rooted in a national context and from the late 1970s it has gradually been internationalised. Secondly, it is assumed that the appearance of satellite technology has been decisive for the development of transnational television services. In the technological deterministic version of this argument, satellite technology is seen as a *sufficient* condition for the spread of transnational TV channels: when the distribution technology was ready, the programmes and the institutional structures followed almost automatically. The more advanced version of the technology argument considers the satellite technology to be only a *necessary* condition for the proliferation of transnational television services. Satellite technology is seen as one among several factors behind the transnationalisation of television.

These assumptions are not quite correct. Radio and television did not begin as national media, and satellite technology has been neither a necessary nor a sufficient condition for the transnationalisation of television in Europe. Television has from its very start been an international medium. Neither in relation to technology, institutional structure nor conventions of expression does it make much sense to call radio and television national media. Television was developed simultaneously in several countries, and the final social form of the medium was to a very large extent a transnational standard. When, for example, Danish television was established in the late 1940s, the Danish TV pioneers travelled around Europe and the United States to learn 'how to make television'. And throughout the history of television there has been an extensive borrowing, copying and adaptation of work methods, technology, means of expression etc. between the national TV services. Rather than calling it a national TV model, it is more correct to speak about a (North) Western European television model and an American television model – each with its own technical standard, institutional structure and conventions of expression. The differences between national TV practices must be considered as variations within the same basic transnational model.

The content of television has also to a large extent been of a transnational character. A considerable amount of the programming in public service television has been foreign material, most obviously the fiction programmes brought from the USA. To this one must add the 'truly' transnational programmes, those programmes produced and simultaneously distributed and broadcast in a number of countries, for instance the live transmission of such international events as the Olympic Games, official ceremonies etc. In television's childhood these kinds of international programmes made up, relatively, a greater proportion of the programmes than today. Partly as a result of insufficient recording possibilities, many TV programmes were exchanged and broadcast simultaneously in several European countries.

The institutional and technological structure which made this transnational television activity possible was the European Broadcasting Union, the EBU, and its television distribution system, Eurovision. Under the influence of the Cold War, the European broadcasting structure was divided into two blocks: OIRT/Intervision, consisting of the East European broadcasting institutions; and EBU/Eurovision, consisting of the Western European and North African broadcasting institutions. The EBU was formed in 1950, and a few years later the exchange of TV programmes began in what later became known as the Eurovision system. In Eurovision, programmes were exchanged free of charge, and this was the first attempt by the public service broadcasters to reduce the costs of TV production. At the same time Eurovision played an important role as supplier of attractive TV programmes in order to stimulate TV sales.

The first 'Summer Season of European Television Exchange' took place from 6 June to 4 July 1954 and was supported by the manufacturers of TV equipment. For instance, Philips included the Eurovision Exchange schedule in their advertisements in order to encourage the sale of TV sets. This first big Eurovision exchange, involving eight countries, culminated in the Football World Cup. The exchange was arranged and announced as a separate European programme of a month's duration. The Eurovision exchange of programmes, especially sport, has continued to grow ever since. In the beginning special European programme series like *The Rivers of Europe* were produced within the exchange framework. Later, the exchanged programmes were more integrated into the national TV programme schedule. The Eurovision fanfare and logo indicated the European origin, but apart from this the Eurovision programmes were not very different from national programmes.

In 1958, the first experiments with the exchange of television news pictures began. This was the beginning of the Eurovision News Exchange that ever since has handled an increasing amount of television news traffic both within Western Europe and between Europe and other continents. Today, Eurovision News Exchange forms the European nerve-centre of TV news; and, with a possible fusion between Intervision and Eurovision as a result of the changes in Eastern Europe, this system will be the dominating infrastructure for TV news for the whole European continent.

It is interesting to note that when the Eurovision experiment began it was called the 'European Newsreel'. This does not only reflect the fact that TV news had not definitively found its own form at this time; it also indicates that the final form of the news exchange was not settled. Initially, some professionals thought of the exchange as the beginning of a separate European television news bulletin. However, the European news items very quickly became integrated into national news bulletins. At the time the experiments were carried out, suggestions were also made about the creation of a European television news agency within the framework of the EBU as a counter-measure to the emerging private TV news agencies, BCINA (Visnews), UPITN (WTN) and others. This idea was never implemented, perhaps because it primarily reflected a French desire to create a European (read French-dominated) alternative to the Anglo-American agencies. The idea of a European television programme and/or news bulletin did not gain a foothold within the EBU, but it continued to show up at regular intervals. In a quite rudimentary form this ambition has survived in such programmes as the 'Eurovision Song Contest', the regular transmission from the Vatican at New Year, etc.

I call attention to these aspects of television's history in order to stress the fact that a pan-European television service or transnational television in general has been a technical possibility since the middle of the 1950s. Describing television's history as simply a move from a national to an international context does not take into account the fact that television also had an early international history. Television was not initially a national medium, but it gradually became 'nationalised' during the 50s and 60s. Then in the late 70s it again became internationalised. It must also be stressed that the national public service institutions since the early 50s have maintained and developed European cooperation in technology, legal matters and programmes.

The national character of television is not a result of the limited range of the television signal; this problem was solved with the Eurovision network more than thirty years ago. When TV satellites play a role in the transnationalisation of television, it is because they are able to provide a considerable increase in distribution capacity. But since the mid–50s it has been technically possible to have a European TV channel besides the national TV channels. The national character of television is a result of political, institutional and to some extent aesthetic factors. The idea of a 'European Newsreel' did not gain ground because political power was almost entirely located at the national level. Although the immediate post-war Europe shared many hopes and ideas of more extensive European and international cooperation, the exercise of political power, the parliamentary institutions and the public sphere remained tied to the national level. Representation of a public sphere had to accommodate this political reality. The national foundation of the broadcasting institutions created an institutional barrier against a European programme. The national institutions did not want to give up authority to any supranational organisation such as the EBU. The predominant attitude among EBU members has been that the EBU should provide a service for the national members and not act as a broadcaster itself besides or above national broadcasters.

Aesthetic problems also created a barrier for the creation of a European TV news programme. In the 1940s and 1950s the aesthetic form of the TV news genre was not fully developed and formats from radio news and the newsreel were still used. These old formats could be used without much difficulty in a multilingual environment like Europe. Spoken news with or without pictures simply required translation as long as the newsreader did not appear in vision. When the TV news format with its extended use of 'talking heads' was introduced, TV news became limited to a single-language environment. Dubbing a news anchor produces an unsatisfactory result which destroys the illusion of the anchor's personal mode of address. An alternative was – and is – subtitling, but this is not common practice outside the Scandinavian countries.

From 'Eurikon' to 'Euronews'

It is possible to distinguish three main types of actors involved in the creation of pan-European television services. First, there are the private TV companies, which are often part of multimedia conglomerates and have been engaged in various transnational TV projects, including TV services aimed at a Europe-wide audience. Second, there are the national public service institutions, which individually, in groups, and together within the framework of the EBU have taken various initiatives of this kind. And third, the European political institutions: the European Council, the European Commission and the European Parliament. I shall concentrate on the last two groups, since the initiatives of the private companies in the field of transnational television are, if not well analysed, at least well described elsewhere.

The first transnational TV project in which the EBU was involved was 'Eurikon' in 1982. The immediate occasion for the EBU's role was an offer from the European Space Agency which allowed the EBU to use the Agency's satellite OTS – the Orbital Test Satellite – to experiment without charge with a pan-European television programme for a direct broadcasting satellite (DBS). Fifteen EBU members officially participated in the 'Eurikon' experiment, but the real participants were ARD (West Germany), NOS (Netherlands), ORF (Austria), RAI (Italy) and the IBA (UK). These five participants each coordinated a week of television programming on the OTS satellite. Since it was only an experiment, the programmes were transmitted by closed circuit and viewed only by the TV staff involved and invited audiences. The programmes comprised both information and entertainment, and each week there were experiments with language (dubbing, subtitling), programme composition, programme presentation etc.

After the 'Eurikon' experiment, the EBU again received an offer from the European Space Agency which made it possible to continue this activity on a more permanent basis. When the Agency's more powerful DBS satellite 'Olympus' was launched, the EBU was given the opportunity to use it without charge for three years for a European programme. To prepare for such a programme, a number of EBU members formed a consortium which initially used a transponder on an ECS satellite. Behind this project, called 'Europa TV', were ARD (West Germany), NOS (Netherlands), RTE (Ireland), RAI (Italy) and RTP (Portugal). 'Europa TV' was aimed at a Europe-wide audience and carried a broad mix of programmes. The channel broadcast continuously from 5 October 1985 to 28 November 1986, when the consortium went into liquidation.

After the cessation of 'Europa TV', the EBU had no realistic project to make use of the access to the Olympus satellite and the agreement with the European Space Agency was cancelled. This did not, however, lead to a general abandonment of plans for a European programme. Instead of trying to establish a new TV channel with a broad mix of programmes, the EBU chose to specialise in sports and news because of its long experience in these fields. The result was the TV satellite channel 'Eurosport', which began broadcasting in February 1989, and the planned TV satellite channel 'Euronews'.

'Eurosport' was initially a consortium of sixteen EBU members and the private company News International. As a consortium of EBU members, 'Eurosport' has achieved member status and has gained access to the exchange of sports programmes.[4] This limits problems of an editorial nature. The EBU as such is not responsible for the programming, but acts as a supplier of programme material. This collaboration with a commercial partner has to be seen in the light of the failure of 'Europa TV', after which EBU members did not want to initiate projects involving a high financial risk. Further, sports programmes are relatively non-controversial, which makes the financial arrangements and the choice of partners fairly unproblematic and does not raise questions of the editorial independence of commercial interests. In the case of 'Euronews', a set-up like this could be more problematic.

The 'Eurosport' channel has nevertheless given rise to controversy. Some national TV stations are beginning to see 'Eurosport' as a competitor. And the very institutional structure has been contested by the European Commission, which sees the close connection between the copyright holder, the distribution system and the broadcaster as a violation of the Treaty of Rome's rules about free competition. The intervention of the European Commission resulted from a complaint by the competing sports channel 'Screensport'.

'Eurosport' must be seen primarily as a practical way for the EBU to make use of the enormous number of sports programmes for which it has acquired international copyright but for which EBU members are unable to make room in their national programme schedules. Because of the one-sidedness and entertainment character of 'Eurosport's programmes, this channel cannot be considered as the public service institutions' contribution to the European dimension in television. 'Eurosport' does not satisfy the wish of the European political institutions for a pan-European television channel. Such a channel must in some way articulate a European political space, and this demands above all a news service as an important part of a European programme.

The different plans for a news service within the framework of the EBU have culminated in the 'Euronews' project. 'Euronews' is planned to be a special channel for news and current affairs. It has been on its way for some years and has been postponed several times. Not all EBU members have been in favour of the project and only some members have engaged actively in the preparations. The active participants are the national broadcasters in Austria, Belgium, Finland, Egypt, France, Germany, Greece, Italy, Jordan, Spain, Turkey and Yugoslavia. The United Kingdom and most of the Nordic countries, for example, do not want to participate in the project, at least for the moment.

The initial plan is for 'Euronews' to broadcast news nine hours a day, from 1600 to 0100 CET. Later, it will extend the transmissions to a 24-hour service. It will broadcast in five languages: English, French, German, Italian and Spanish. Off-screen commentary and subtitling will be used extensively in order to minimise the involvement of traditional newsreaders because of the inherent language problems. During the day the programme will consist of short news flashes (of approximately five minutes) every half hour, with current affairs programmes in between. In the evening, more extensive news bulletins (of approximately thirty minutes) will begin every half hour. The main source for 'Euronews' will be the news pictures from the Eurovision News Exchange. The 'Euronews' channel will have its own staff of journalists and editors but it will not gather news itself. It will be very dependent on the coverage provided by EBU members.

The EBU presented the project to the European Commission in February 1991, applying to the EC and other European institutions for 10 million ECU a year in order to set up and operate the channel until 1996. The EBU itself will contribute to the project by giving 'Euronews' free access to the Eurovision News Exchange. EBU members actively involved in 'Euronews' will contribute 2.3 million

ECU a year. The remaining cost will be financed by advertising. The EBU has not, as in the case of 'Eurosport', involved a commercial partner in the 'Euronews' project. 'Euronews' is seen as a major contribution from the public service institutions to the European dimension in television, and its purpose is to demonstrate the indispensability of the public service concept. In relation to news, the aim is to stress the necessity of the public service idea as a guarantee of independence, impartiality, quality etc. This excludes collaboration with commercial TV companies: 'Euronews' is dependent on financial support from the European political institutions.

Changing and Conflicting Interests
The EBU's engagement in pan-European television projects has been driven by three main interests. To begin with, the EBU and its members wanted to gain experience with DBS technology. The EBU has always been the forum in which the European TV institutions have exchanged and developed experience with new TV technologies and the inherent changes in programme possibilities and legal and administrative procedures. The 'Eurikon' experiment was a good opportunity for all EBU members to gain experience with DBS technology irrespective of whether members wanted to develop a pan-European television programme or introduce their own transnational TV projects. Secondly, EBU members wanted to be able to compete more directly with the transnational commercial newcomers. By countering the competitors on both a national and a transnational level, the EBU could be used to gain competitive advantage. Thirdly, the different pan-European TV projects have been an occasion for the EBU to acquire political and financial goodwill and support from the European political institutions.

During the 1980s the role of the EBU was transformed. Earlier it was simply the union of European broadcasters, a forum of the professional expertise within the field; increasingly, the EBU has become an interest group of public service broadcasters, and as such it represents only one of the different groupings in the broadcasting industry. In the same period the European political institutions, and especially the European Commission, have begun to play a much more active role in the regulation of the European media structure. As a result of this parallel development, it has become important for the EBU to acquire the recognition of the European political institutions as a central and indispensable part of the audiovisual industry. Earlier this position was a matter of course – there were no other broadcasters; now it is something constantly to be achieved and sustained. As a result, pan-European TV projects are for the EBU more a means of achieving political recognition than an end in themselves.

During the 1980s a displacement of interest took place. In the first half of the decade it was primarily the first interest – gaining experience with DBS technology – that was important for the EBU. In the second half of the 1980s this has given way to other concerns: more direct competition with the commercial newcomers and, especially, the achievement of recognition from the European political institutions. The problems of DBS technology are no longer a key issue.

This displacement of interest is, as already mentioned, a result of the altered relationship between the EBU and the European political institutions. The Council of Europe has been involved in questions of media policy from a very early stage, and the EBU has had close collaboration with it. The EC institutions, however, became involved in media matters much later. The first initiative from an EC institution originated with the European Parliament. On the one hand they were concerned with the creation of a pan-European television programme in order to strengthen European integration; on the other, they recommended initiatives to ensure freedom of thought, protection of children against violence and pornography etc., as counter-measures to the increased commercialisation and transnationalisation of the media.

The first initiatives from the European Parliament concerning the creation of a pan-European programme also received support from the European Commission, and for the practical implementation of such a project the participation of the EBU was considered essential.[5] This unqualified support for the EBU was, however, also based on pragmatic considerations. At this point the EBU and its members were among the very few broadcasters with practical experience in this field. The alternative – the creation of a new, independent European public service institution – was considered too expensive and would create legal and political problems.[6]

Although a pan-European television service continued to have priority, from the middle of the 1980s other interests and initiatives began to dominate the media agenda of the EC institutions. The European Commission's 1984 Green Paper, *Television without Frontiers*, took a much more economic approach to media policy, and in the following years it was the removal of barriers for the free flow and exchange of media products across national borders that preoccupied the Commission. The media sector was going to be an integral part of the single market. Then followed the MEDIA project and later Audiovisual Eureka, both aimed at the formation of a more integrated Western European audiovisual industry.

In the course of this political development the European Commission's positive attitude towards the EBU declined. Influenced by a narrow economic approach to media policy and neo-conservative deregulation policies in general, the Commission lent credence to the notion of the private sector as a centre of growth, and the EBU became associated – in the eyes of the Commission – with the old order of public monopolies and national protectionism. The Eurovision system also fell into disfavour with the Commission, which considered it a cartel preventing free competition and as such a violation of the Treaty of Rome. The EBU was forced to change the rules of access to the Eurovision network and allow non-members, that is commercial TV stations, to have access under special conditions to the programme and news exchanges. The alternative could have been the dissolution of the Eurovision system.

This development changed the relative balance of power between the EBU and the European political institutions. During the 'Eurikon' experiment, the EBU could take advantage of the support from the European institutions without really paying attention to the wishes of these institutions. This is no longer the case. At the time when 'Europa TV' was under consideration, concern was already being expressed about the reaction of the EC institutions if the EBU was unable to create a European TV channel. The EBU's worry was primarily that the EC would give the task to someone else. For example, the international TV news agency Visnews had asked the European Community for financial support for the planning of a European TV news channel, and the 1984 Arfé report had considered this channel to be a good complement to the EBU's 'Europa TV' project.[7] When 'Europa TV' failed and the EBU had no alternative projects, the EC institutions expressed 'disappointment'. As a result, the EBU's Administrative Council asked its programme committee to develop new plans for a European programme. The outcome was the 'Eurosport' and 'Euronews' projects.

As a result of the Commission's unfavourable attitude towards the EBU and the generally defensive position of the public service broadcasters, the EBU increasingly tries to use the plans for a European programme as a means of regaining for public service broadcasting some of its former credibility. More specifically, the aim is to ensure that the interests of the EBU and its members are taken into proper consideration in the regulation of the European media structure and in the elaboration of the different European audiovisual projects. When the French government and the EC Commission together launched Audiovisual Eureka, 'the 'Euronews' project was an important asset with which the EBU could promote itself.

This short summary of the political situation reflects a more general political tendency at the beginning of the 1990s. The 'ultra-liberal' deregulation policy is, if not reversed, then at least in decline at both the national and the European level. The deregulation policy, even when evaluated by its own narrow economic criteria, has reached its own limit. The assumption that leaving still more activities to the market would create new growth in the audiovisual sector and as a result decrease dependence on the United States has turned out to be insufficient. Deregulation policies have increased the number of distribution channels, but the production of software has not been able to keep up with the distribution capacity. In effect the software dependency on the United States has increased. At the end of the 1980s the EC institutions initiated comprehensive development programmes for the audiovisual industry and at the same time implemented different measures in order to protect the European market against the USA's media industry (the import quota recommendations of the EC directive on transnational television, for example).

Behind this recognition of the limitations of deregulation policies is also an acknowledgment of the fact that the old national public service institutions have adjusted themselves to the new conditions and are likely to be an important part of the national and transnational television structure for many years. The 1980s have also shown that the commercial newcomers are not capable of setting up a pan-European television service. A number of commercial satellite TV projects aimed at a European audience ended up as financial disasters. Instead satellite TV has become regionalised, typically aimed at language communities: a German-speaking audience, a French audience, a Scandinavian audience etc. This implies that – in the eyes of the European political institutions – the EBU is the organisation that is most likely to be able to carry out a pan-European programme.

Internal Disagreements
After the 'Eurikon' experiment the elaboration of the programme structure and journalistic standards of a European news programme was left to the journalistic forum of the EBU, the Television News Working Party (TNWP). This Working Party, which meets twice a year, gathers senior journalists from all the national TV stations. On several occasions the TNWP has discussed the possibility of a joint news service within the EBU framework. But the majority has

always been very sceptical. For example, it was suggested in 1984 that the TNWP should form a sort of editorial committee to strengthen the co-production of news and current affairs programmes about international events of common interest, like elections to the European Parliament. The deliberation of this idea was carried so far that an internal pilot for such a programme was produced. Reactions from the majority of the journalistic representatives were unfavourable to the idea.

The basic view in this forum of senior TV journalists has been that the EBU and its different committees and working parties should not have any editorial responsibilities but should act only as a forum for co-operation between independent national news services. Furthermore, a definition of Europe making it synonymous with the countries of the European Community has never been acceptable because EBU members come from the whole of Western Europe as well as North Africa and the Middle East.

Nevertheless, the TNWP did engage in the elaboration of the structure and principles for a European news programme to be distributed via satellite. The higher institutional considerations have made it difficult for the journalistic forum to reject the idea completely. And, it must be added, some of the journalistic representatives have been in favour of such plans. In February 1984 the TNWP formed an ad hoc sub-group to study the financing and production of a European news programme and sketch out the basic policy, including the journalistic standards to be applied to such a programme. Of fundamental interest are the proposed guidelines for a 'programming philosophy' for a pan-European news programme (see Appendix to this essay). These editorial guidelines reflect traditional journalistic principles about impartiality, objectivity, independence of commercial and political interests etc. The guidelines also include specifications whose primary objectives are to avoid both interference from the European political institutions and a narrow definition of Europe:

> Europe is defined geographically in this context as all countries with an EBU active member (the European Broadcasting area) and is not to be confused with political frontiers. ... [The news programme] should not attempt to create common European viewpoints or a European outlook on events but, on the contrary, should simply reflect the different European views in as impartial and balanced a way as possible, as well as reflecting the political, economic, ethnic, religious and cultural pluralism within the European population.[8]

As regards the European dimension, a very wide definition of Europe is chosen and the importance of pluralism is stressed. These principles express the traditional scepticism in the TNWP towards a European news programme, and in particular the fear that an EBU news programme should become the voice of the EC. At the same time the proposal can be considered a compromise between the representatives in favour of a European programme and the absolute opponents in the TNWP. These principles have been considered again in relation to the 'Euronews' project. They do not, however, represent an official EBU policy but can be said to express the prevailing attitude of the TNWP. Until now they represent the most elaborated ideas of a news philosophy for a European news programme.

The planning of the 'Euronews' project has to a large extent taken place outside the journalistic forum of the EBU. It has moved higher up in the EBU hierarchy as a result of the project's importance for the general policy of the EBU and probably also because of the TNWP's scepticism about the project. Some members of the journalistic forum fear that the political motives behind the 'Euronews' project could limit editorial independence and give the news programme an outlook influenced by the political agenda of the EC institutions. These worries among the journalistic representatives have not been given the same importance as the 'higher' policy considerations.

In addition to fundamental disagreements about the structure and purpose of 'Euronews', there have also been complications of a practical nature and interest conflicts of a more narrow character. During the 1980s the national public service institutions have experienced financial cutbacks, and are therefore not able to use large resources on projects not closely related to their central activity and which involve a considerable financial risk. In some countries there are political and/or legal problems in using the licence fee for a programme activity which has no national aim and will be distributed in such a way (satellite and cable) that it will not be accessible for all. Controversy also stems from the fact that the 'Euronews' channel will compete with national news programmes. In the proposed programme schedule this problem has been taken into consideration by placing five-minute news slots and current affairs programmes during the day; the regular news programmes, with a duration of thirty minutes, are scheduled in the evening. This structure reduces the incentive of the audience to use 'Euronews' as an alternative to national news programmes during the day, but 'Euronews' will nevertheless pose a problem for national broadcasters.

86

Some of the big national broadcasters have transnational TV programmes of their own, and these could also be affected by EBU projects. These transnational TV projects had implications for the 'Europa TV' project because the EBU members, instead of giving priority to 'Europa TV', concentrated their efforts on their own transnational satellite projects.

The political disagreement in the EBU about the 'Euronews' project must be considered a healthy sign. It indicates that a debate about fundamental political and journalistic principles is taking place. One can only regret that the discussions are rather limited, and – not least – closed to a wider public. Let me now point to the weaknesses in the arguments of both supporters and sceptics where a European news programme is concerned.

The proponents of 'Euronews' tend to ignore the fact that there is a real danger of editorial dependence on the European political institutions. The combination of direct financial dependence and the more indirect political dependence stemming from the EBU's interest in being on good terms with the European political institutions can make it difficult to sustain and develop an independent and critical journalism. However, this dependence is not different from the kind of dependence the public service broadcasters have experienced for decades at the national level. And a European channel will have the advantage of not being legally or politically responsible to the European political institutions.

The opponents of the EBU's involvement in 'Euronews' ignore the fact that any news programme must relate itself to a demarcated political and social sphere and refer to the political institutions within this sphere. The national news programmes do this, as do transnational news channels like Sky News and CNN. Furthermore they tend to overlook the fact that news coverage of the EC institutions does not need to be propaganda for these institutions or arguments for further integration. Correspondingly, coverage of national political questions being debated in parliament or government does not necessarily legitimise these political institutions or serve as an argument for giving them greater authority.

A European Political Public Sphere?

A European TV news programme will become part of a still incomplete European political sphere, and will at the same time contribute to the formation of such a sphere. In order to reflect on this theoretically, I will discuss the applicability of Habermas's theory of the public sphere. I have chosen Habermas's theory because it has already had a strong influence on Continental media research, especially in Germany and the Nordic countries, and lately it has also influenced British media research. The English translation of Habermas is likely to increase this influence.[9]

To begin with, I will warn against an uncritical use of Habermas's categories for the analysis of public structures created by the mass media. Habermas's theory of the structural transformation of the public sphere, which I presuppose known, suffers from many deficiencies and can only be made useful through a major adaptation. The fundamental problem is that the development of the public sphere from the nineteenth century until 1961 (when the book was written) is conceived solely in terms of decline. The public sphere between the state and the private world decreases as a result of the overlapping of state and civil society, and the free citizen's rational discussion of public matters disappears. The old, ideal type of public sphere gives rise to the mass media's manipulated representation of a political debate, and the democratic process becomes increasingly influenced by interest groups and bureaucratic work processes. The citizens no longer participate in public debate, but increasingly attend as passive observers whose function is to provide acclamation of the exercise of political power. As for the role of the mass media, they are only regarded as an instrument for the 'refeudalisation' of society. Habermas does not distinguish between commercial and publicly regulated media; they are all part of a manipulated publicity which gradually transforms the political citizen into a private consumer. Habermas's view of the mass media is marked by the same pessimism which characterised early critical theory, and places itself within the traditional dichotomy between high and low culture.

By exclusively focusing on decline, Habermas tends to ignore the fact that a very significant increase in democratic rights and possibilities has taken place in the same period. The classic bourgeois public sphere, which Habermas puts forward as an ideal, rested – like the democracy of Athens – on the systematic exclusion of the majority of the population from political influence. Access to the public sphere was limited by virtue of property, education or gender. Although many inequalities continue to exist, the extension of the right to vote, the expansion of public education, the spread of mass media and more generally the growth of the social welfare state have resulted in a massive increase in formal as well as actual democratic possibilities.

Habermas's ideal of a public sphere has an ambiguous connection to the development of democracy. He does not give full priority to the question of democracy because his main interest is to identify the conditions for a rational communication unaffected by power relations. He locates these conditions in the early classical public sphere, in spite of the fact that this structure can hardly be said to have been democratic when considered in a general social context. It can further be asked whether this classical public sphere, which Habermas seeks to identify, was a historical reality or the ideal for which the early bourgeoisie strived. Habermas seems to use the early bourgeoisie's own ideal of democracy as a yardstick for historical development. The democratic 'idyll' he locates in early bourgeois society is only revealed in his selection of historical evidence to confirm his theory.

To use Habermas for a contemporary analysis of mass media the concepts of *representation* and *interest* must be given a new meaning and function. Whereas Habermas presupposes that participation is the only proper way to engage in public life, it must be realised that representation is a necessity. In a mass democracy the democratic process must at some levels have a non-direct character and rest on the representation of viewpoints and arguments. Habermas argues that rational public reasoning presupposes the absence of conflicting interests. In a socially and culturally divided society, however, it is necessary that conflicting and even antagonistic interests are represented in the public sphere. Representation must rest on a fundamental pluralism which gives access to divergent interests. Only by making the actual social contradictions and the multitude of viewpoints visible is it possible to create the conditions for a rational public debate and a democratic political process.

In the past, public service broadcasting tried to achieve representation without pluralism. Opinions and information were selected according to whether or not they conformed to the consensus of the dominant national political culture. As a result, public service broadcasting neglected the political, social and aesthetic experience of different social groupings and classes.[10] A revitalisation of the public service concept must take pluralism as its starting point.

These objections to Habermas's theory apply even more to a transnationalised public sphere. The difference in scale means that the relation between participation and representation will be radically different. In a national context it is possible to maintain a closer relation between participation and representation. At least in principle, it is possible for everybody to have access to the public sphere, including the media, and to represent themselves. This is inevitably an illusion in a European public sphere. The representation of such a sphere will be managed by professionals, journalists, politicians, opinion-makers etc. The number of different interests claiming the right to be represented will multiply at the European level, thus making a consensus even more difficult to establish.

Habermas's description of the transformation of the public sphere is misleading when applied to the national level. His critique of the character of the present political public sphere does, however, make good sense when applied to the transnational, European level. The deficiencies of the European public sphere are, however, not the result of a decline, but the effect of an unequal development in which the internationalisation of capital and the formation of a supra-state administration and regulation have grown rapidly but have not been accompanied by a parallel development of public knowledge. This has given cause to the debate about the 'democratic deficit' of the EC institutions, but perhaps Habermas's concept of (re)feudalisation is a more precise characterisation of the present European political structure.

The real political decision-making process has disappeared from the public space and is carried out by EC officials and politicians in collaboration with the transnational industry and different interest groups. Only on special occasions does the public have the opportunity to sit in on the political process, not in order to represent arguments or viewpoints but only to witness the exercise of political authority. At the European level there is no public with the ability to perform a critical function or represent alternative interpretations or definitions of the political agenda. The national public sphere and the national political institutions are not geared to exercise such a transnational publicity. In practice it is difficult even for the members of the national parliaments to keep pace with developments at the European level. In effect the European political institutions do not have to legitimise their decisions and actions to the same extent as their national counterparts.

A European public sphere is only in its infancy, and it is not obvious what demarcates this sphere, since Europe is changing size and character. More and more countries are applying for membership of the EC, and this breaks the exclusivity of the club. The changes in Eastern and Central Europe show a Europe both becoming bigger and disintegrating as new national minorities claim their right to independence. This also changes the size and nature of the European political institutions. A European political sphere cannot have the same character as its national counterpart. The establishment of a critical journalism must take the very unstable character of the European dimension and the unclarified legitimacy of the European political institutions as its point of departure.

The institutions involved in the representation of a European sphere will, in the nature of the case, be highly professionalised and centralised and as such will tend to elude criticism of their own practice. If this representation is left to the market, there will be no institutional structure to ensure a public debate about the very exercise of public political communication. In the market, only an indirect criticism will be exercised, through the consumer's use of the 'off' button. A critical debate about the exercise of journalism requires an institutional construction which creates a public debate about the internal practice of media institutions. The media institutions themselves must be subjected to a demand that both their employees and the general public have the opportunity to question the practice of representation. As mentioned earlier, such an internal critique has been exercised with the EBU structure in the case of 'Euronews', but only to a limited extent and only among the broadcasters themselves.

Pan-European Television News: Final Considerations

The 'Euronews' project has inherent problems. Being a collaboration between national broadcasters, it must be careful not to compete directly with the national TV broadcasters' news programmes. This could turn out to be a serious disadvantage in the competition with other transnational news channels. The disagreements in the EBU about what is to be understood by the European dimension could give cause to a changeable news policy and distrust of the credibility of the news service.

These weaknesses could, however, also turn out to be the strength of the 'Euronews' channel. The discussions in the EBU about the different interpretations of the European dimension and journalistic philosophy in general could ensure that the 'Euronews' programme will not only be determined by market considerations and/or pressure from the EC institutions but will also be subject to political considerations. The fact that the EBU consists of publicly regulated institutions makes the institutions – at least in principle – more likely to be responsive to public criticism. The 'Euronews' channel maintains, through the EBU, its relation to the national news services, and this could imply that the outlook of the news programme will not be as much *pan*-European as *multi*-national and *trans*-national. A very concrete effect of this multi-national dimension is the multilingual service of 'Euronews'. The audience will have access to international news in many different languages, in many cases their own, and not only in English as in the case of CNN and Sky News.

The fact that 'Euronews' must be careful not to compete directly with national news programmes could imply that its news service will be different from the rather superficial news coverage provided by CNN and Sky News. The great number of current affairs programmes which are to be broadcast in the daytime could provide a much more varied and thorough treatment of international developments. The aforementioned crisis of representation forces the broadcasting institutions to consider the very legitimacy of their work. At best this could result in a news service in which a critical attitude prevails not only in the traditional journalistic meaning of the word, but also as a critical reflection of news values in relation to different interpretations of the European dimension.

It is, of course, not possible to say with certainty in which direction a project like 'Euronews' will move. Perhaps 'Euronews' will provide critical coverage of international developments for a European audience, but it could also end up as a toothless communicator of the political agenda of the EC institutions.

The institutional structures which will exercise political communication on a European level are about to take shape. Until now, media research has analysed the European media development on a more general level. It is necessary, however, that concrete audiovisual projects too are subjected to close analysis. In this way media research can perform a more direct critical function in the formation of a European political public sphere.

Appendix
Below are the recommendations for a pan-European news programming philosophy made by the ad hoc sub-group of the EBU Television News Working Party. The guidelines are not official adopted EBU policy but represent the viewpoint of the ad hoc group (TNWP).

– the programme should be of an obvious transnational European flavour. The items must be relevant to the 'European audience'. One of the most important criteria for the selection of stories should be the degree to which the viewers are affected or interested by the importance and repercussions of an event;
– Europe is defined geographically in this context as all countries with an EBU active member (the European Broadcasting area) and is not to be confused with political frontiers;
– the news reporting must be factual, credible and reliable. All sources must imperatively be checked, thus necessitating a staff

capable of operating efficiently in a neutral and objective manner;
- the programme must be completely unbiased and should not promote any political or ideological views;
- the programme should not attempt to create common European viewpoints or a European outlook on events but, on the contrary, should simply reflect the different European views in as impartial and balanced a way as possible, as well as reflecting the political, economic, ethnic, religious and cultural pluralism within the European population. The European newsroom should channel its efforts towards gathering points of view rather than making them;
- bearing in mind the pluralistic concept of the programme, the European newsroom should collaborate closely with and be assisted by the relevant national newsrooms, instead of attempting to tackle a given topic wholly by itself. Whilst the central European desk would present the facts, ideally the national newsrooms and their reporters would be called upon to provide explanations to the viewers;
- the EBU organisation as a whole with its existing framework is considered the most competent body to further cooperation in this field with the well established resources at its disposal;
- in accordance with the traditional role of public broadcasters in Europe, the programme must be totally independent of any national or international political pressure and/or must not be influenced by trade and industry. Should external funds be considered necessary they would be acceptable only if editorial independence was completely unaffected;
- the responsibilities of the editorial staff and its chief editor should be determined within the structure of an editorial statute. The chief editor would be responsible only to the governing board (i.e. once per quarter and retroactively);
- the sub-group declared that in practical terms a heterogeneous team (editors from different European nations) would be preferable to a homogeneous production unit (an agency or broadcaster) and stressed the importance of heading the multinational team with a highly independent chief editor. Staff on secondment from their national newsrooms would be responsible only to the chief editor and not to their home organisations.

Quoted from 'Pan-European News Programme', meetings of the TV News Working Party's Sub-Group, Divonne, 12 November 1984, Geneva, 3 December 1984, reproduced in EBU document SPG 3862, March 1985, annex 18.

Notes

1. See D. Cardiff, P. Scannell, 'Serving the Nation: Public Service Broadcasting before the War', in B. Waite *et al.* (eds.), *Popular Culture: Past and Present* (London: Croom Helm, 1982); P. Scannell, 'Public Service Broadcasting: The History of a Concept', in A. Goodwin, G. Whannel (eds.), *Understanding Television* (London: Routledge, 1990).
2. R. Williams, *Towards 2000* (London: Chatto and Windus/Hogarth Press, 1983), p. 197.
3. N. Garnham, *Capitalism and Communication: Global Culture and the Economics of Information* (London: Sage, 1990), p. 114.
4. News International withdrew from the Eurosport consortium in April 1991, and has since been replaced by TF1, the main French commercial channel (eds.).
5. See 'Realities and tendencies in European Television: Perspectives and Options'. Interim report from the Commission to the European Parliament, COM(83) 229 Final, 25 May 1983.
6. See the Hahn report on behalf of the Committee on Youth, Culture, Education, Information and Sport, 23 February 1982, PE73.271/Final.
7. The Arfé Report, on behalf of the Committee on Youth, Culture, Education, Information and Sport, 16 March 1984, PE85.902/Final.
8. EBU Document SPG 2805, Appendix 11, March 1985, describing meetings of the TV News Working Party's Sub-Group, Pan-European News Programme, 12 November and 3 December 1984.
9. J. Habermas, *Strukturwandel der Öffentlichkeit: Untersuchungen zu einer Kategorie der bürgerlichen Gesellschaft* (Berlin: Herman Luchterhand Verlag, 1962); translated as *The Structural Transformation of the Public Sphere* (Ann Arbor: MIT Press, 1989).
10. See A. Kluge, O. Negt, *Öffentlichkeit und Erfahrung: Zur Organisationsanalyse von bürgerlicher und proletarischer Öffentlichkeit* (Frankfurt-am-Main: Suhrkamp Verlag, 1972); D. Prokop, *Faszination und Langweile: Die populären Medien* (Stuttgart: dtv Wissenschaft, 1979).

National Policy and the Traded Image

Toby Miller

From the time of its emergence as one of the key trading and monet-
ary protocols of the late 1940s until the shifts and shocks of the
1970s, the GATT (General Agreement on Tariffs and Trade) enshrined the key principles of the world trading system: multilatera-
lism, non-discrimination, and codified methods of regulation in
place of sovereign administrative discretion on the part of individual
states. It became the bureaucratic champion of free trade, dedicated
to the removal of blocks to the 'natural' operation of a perfect market
organised around the preferred rhythms of supply and demand
under the intersecting signs of pure comparative advantage and consumer sovereignty.

This was very much the United States' agenda and it worked well
until the appearance of the European Community (EC) and Japan as
fields of real economic force. This effect was doubled by some
internal loss of faith that a liberal trading regime necessarily coincided with the best interests of the USA. By the 1980s, international
debates on trade were based on the binary opposites of liberalism
and mercantilism, but with no major player staking lofty moral
terrain other than on a contingent, site-specific basis; protectionism
was accepted when it worked for the speaking subject, rejected when
it worked for some other entity to that speaker's detriment.

The GATT has suffered through the very success of its legalism,
which has encouraged resistance via the emergence of new forms of
protectionism appearing as non-tariff implements and, latterly,
industry policy.[1] This comes as no surprise to dissident economists,
who have reacted against the neoclassical model over the last 150
years for its tendentious dependence on 'individual preference order-
ings, endowments, and technology'.[2] In particular, they have noted

that the signified of 'free trade' is the self-interest of the most powerful. US demands for a deregulated domain of cultural openness have been criticised as a form of 'corporate libertarianism' serving particular sets of interests at particular times. There have been significant counter-influences on the US Executive to increase or at least sustain its own protectionism in both agriculture and services. This was possible because the President's authority to strike GATT agreements on these matters is legislated for within sunset clauses and is therefore highly contingent. The US may now be planning a less totalising approach to service industries diplomacy, one that relies on bilateral discussions until and unless the GATT pays dividends. For the moment, however, the Uruguay Round of the GATT has been a critical site for the operation of international cultural policy.

The late 1980s saw a massive expansion in the quantitative importance of trade in services (TIS), with obvious significance for the realm called 'culture'. Prior to this period, it was conventional to downplay the significance of TIS, because of technological limitations and networks of domestic regulation. Traditional co-location of production and consumption militated against the international development of the sector. TIS expressly includes broadcasting, film and television production and distribution within the terms of the GATT. Current negotiations on freeing the sector from market distortion could affect such areas as: legislation by particular sovereign-states for local content quotas in the media; foreign ownership of broadcasters; public subvention of the screen industries; and state assistance given to indigenous bourgeoisies to move into export markets. The problem with active assistance is that it contravenes one of the principal formative elaborations of GATT logic; namely, that forms of state aid should be via tariffs instead of restrictions or non-tariff measures, in order that such distortions to the market are visible, predictable and thus capable of being planned around as well as verified. None of this, of course, denies the desired *telos* of GATT: the eventual elimination of all actions by states that hamper free trade.

The theoretical logic underpinning this critique of state protection of industries is that economies will eventually attain a mutual natural equilibrium if they are organised around already extant (i.e. non-legislated) factor endowments that provide them with a comparative advantage over others. Despite their awareness that this has favoured the already-strong, over ninety sovereign-states are signatories to the 100-plus agreements that make up the GATT. When the US put TIS on the agenda, it threatened to leave the GATT if

96

others rejected the move, coinciding as this did with a decline in the value of traditional, secondary US industrialism, but a clear development of its advantage in the services sector.[3] The culture industries were not included in the Free Trade Agreement with Canada signed in 1988, although representatives of the US Trade Department were lobbying the EC at the same time against the threatened imposition of quotas on TV programmes coming from outside the Community.[4]

The US is especially scathing of the notion of a pan-European culture. After years of supporting European unification, there is now something of a reaction in the light of terrors about what *Forbes* magazine has called 'a protectionist, corporatist, anti-American Frankenstein'.[5] In reality, the proposed limit of 50 per cent of broadcast time devoted to imports would make very little difference to existing practice, with the US currently providing a (sizeable) fraction of this amount. The developing proliferation of stations in the wake of deregulation across Western Europe means that new entrants, faced with high start-up costs, have already shown themselves willing to ignore or abuse any directives on localism in the interests of filling airtime with cheap US product, and this will presumably develop as a trend. At the end of the 1980s, TV in Western Europe was using about 150,000 programme hours a year, a figure expected to rise to 350,000 hours by 1995 because of new technology and deregulation. Lobbyists for the American screen industries and US trade negotiators criticised the EC's *Television without Frontiers* directive for being in direct conflict with GATT principles.

We can gain some sense of the relative dispositions within the GATT on this matter from the August 1990 meeting to discuss the TIS sub-topic document, entitled *Draft Services Trade Framework for Audiovisual Services*. Most states represented in Geneva referred in debate to 'the cultural importance of the audiovisual sector'. India and Canada argued for the addition of a clause which would exempt 'assistance measures imposed for cultural reasons' from *laissez-faire* protocols. The European Community preferred a 'sectoral annotation', which would allow for greater flexibility by permitting space for future assistance measures that might be required to develop various aspects of the audiovisual continuum. Japan and Australia spoke favourably of the need to maintain cultural sovereignty but were non-committal on the specifics of the *Draft*. The United States was unequivocally and implacably opposed to any form of exception or notation. Its negotiating team was quoted as saying that the GATT should 'agree to disagree on motives – cultural sovereignty or business opportunity – and then start negotiating'.[6] There is more than a little irony in this, when one considers that US government diplomacy, information-gathering, quotas and tariffs were critical to the establishment of Hollywood's success in setting internationally attractive cost structures in place and expanding monopolistically through the 1920s; but then history is not the motor of neoclassical discourse. One might, however, have expected a certain amount of reflexivity concerning two decades of generous tax credits for US investors in American film and television, in addition to numerous tax shelter schemes and evidence that US businesses operate a selling cartel each year at the Cannes Festival. In another sense, though, this represented a strong continuity in US policy. During the first GATT negotiations in 1947, it had pushed for free trade in film, inscribed in Article IV of the original Agreement; and the early 1960s had witnessed attempts to have trade restrictions on TV removed.[7]

These positions exist against a backdrop in which there is almost no importation of TV programming by the American networks. In contrast, more than 10 per cent of TV time in Western Europe is taken up with US programmes, and 30 per cent in Canada and Latin America.[8] Drama varies significantly in these statistics. Fiction comprises 37 per cent of European TV schedules, but just a quarter of that is produced locally; American imports account for 44 per cent of the rest. Only the United Kingdom and the former Federal Republic of Germany made more TV than they bought in the 1980s. American balance of payments figures are assisted by an estimated US$500 million a year from television exports, up more than five times on the 1972 dollar value. In 1983 it had 75 per cent of the value of all international television trade, mostly in drama. 1988 brought $US5.5 billion in revenue from overseas sales of entertainment, the nation's second largest earner after the aerospace sector.[9] And between those years, American TV sales to Europe went from $US212 million to $US675 million. Predictions for 1991 suggested that exports of film and TV would generate $US6.7 billion in foreign earnings, up 13 per cent on 1990 and nearly double the 1985 figure. This should be seen in a context in which the US had an overall trade deficit of $US100 billion in 1989, was moving towards being a net importer, and was the world's most indebted nation.

So the stakes in TV were high for the United States government. As its key image market trade paper, *Variety*, put it, the prospects for the 1990s were that 'as old borders come down and old ideologies give way, preach the true believers, the *lingua franca* of motion pictures will command a greater worldwide audience than ever before.'[10] More prosaically, the majority of US television drama was being financed on a deficit basis. Producers were selling programmes to the domestic networks at well below cost, having planned on recoupment and profit through US syndication to domestic stations, allied to sales overseas. What had once been the source of super-profit was now effectively an iterable component in the servicing of debt.

There are important correlative cultural policy views. As Sandra Braman has argued:

> The focus on information as a commodity by the US is part of an overall rejection of cultural, social or political valuation of inter-national information flows that is embedded in background studies for policy-makers, congressional hearings and policy statements in a quite self-conscious way.[11]

The intellectual training ground that might have provided a locus of calculation in this domain was simply absent at the policy and aca-demic level outside critical communications scholarship. Similarly, policy-makers in Europe from the 1950s on had routinely conceived of television as a critical pedagogical instrument in the formation of citizens and the elevation of public taste, primarily via news and current affairs. This officially endorsed genre never proved to be as popular as American entertainment programmes. And even the model of the public broadcaster able to act as a guardian of morality came to be problematised through developments in the spheres of satellite, cable, US marketing and new modes of viewing practice. Public policy has come to recognise that more drama is watched around the world than at any other time in history. And it may well be that the flow of television makes for a transfer of what has been called the 'aura of truth' from news and current affairs to fiction.[12] Quite clearly, this presents a dilemma for cultural policy. It is a dilemma with historical contours wrapped round the development of a series of policy constructions of the United States as the mounte-bank of twentieth-century visual culture.

The International Cultural Order
In 1926, the League of Nations sponsored an International Film Congress to discuss the issue of American dominance of the market, but attempts to act in concert as particular trading blocs against Hollywood failed.[13] The *Daily Express* worried the following year that the exposure of British youth to US entertainment was making them 'temporary American citizens'.[14] This has been an enduring complaint. Nearly sixty years later, the Commission of the European

99

Community was prescribing 'a common market for television production . . . if the dominance of the big American media corporations is to be counterbalanced'.[15]

This might also be read as a reaction to the simple magnitude of the US presence in the global economy. For all its huge debts, America continues to dominate the world economy. In 1989, the 500 biggest multinationals were located in just nineteen urban centres, ten of them in the US. This kind of concentration makes for perceptions of imbalance, particularly when it is allied to an aggressively interventionist and moralistic foreign policy presence. US companies and the US government are conceived as coterminous; and their ideological work is seen to be done through the culture industries.

The development of a cultural imperialism thesis in the 1960s, in Latin America in particular, argued that the US, as the world's leading producer and exporter of television, was transferring its dominant value system to others. There was said to be a corresponding diminution in the vitality and standing of local languages and traditions, and hence a threat to national identity. International organisations, for example UNESCO, became the domain for the mobilisation of these logics by governmental agencies. Third World countries lobbied at a series of meetings and conferences for what has been variously termed a New International Information Order or New World Information and Cultural Order (NWICO), mirroring calls for a New International Economic Order and a revised North–South dialogue. This is a dialogue that is re-envisaged as an ideal speech-act, one where it is possible and indeed necessary for the sovereign-state to supertend relative differentials of economic power and calls for an end to processes of unequal exchange whereby First World countries create and manage markets in other places. What began as a concentration on news flow and the TV presentation of Third World countries has been broadened to include the place of the computer in economic and social development and the allocation of telecommunications frequencies. This has continued to occur under the imprimatur of what was announced at the 1973 meeting of Heads of State of Non-Aligned Countries as 'the need to reaffirm national cultural identity'.

UNESCO was the agency with an infrastructure to implement policies flowing from such a rhetoric, but it has operated from a complex set of imperatives, combining the proclamation of a universal humanity and tolerance that sees culture as singular and inalienable with a more specifically politico-diplomatic drive towards the recognition of difference that obeys the founding dictate of an organisation based on sovereign-states.[16] It has now ceased to be the

100

critical site for NWICO debate, in part perhaps because the Americans withdrew from it in 1984 in the light of the Organisation's 'increasing politicisation'.[17] Australian diplomats have argued that the US chose to debate TIS in the GATT because, as a forum, it 'is not strongly influenced by ideological controversies'.[18] Less developed countries have fought hard to resist the US push for the GATT to open up TIS, both on the grounds of cultural sovereignty and the desirability of establishing their own industrial infrastructure of culture for economic reasons.

But it would be misleading to isolate this – as opposed to the very broad debates on restructuring global inequality – within the domain of the Third World. At 'Mondiacult 1982', the Mexico City world conference on cultural production, Jack Lang, the French Minister for Culture, caused a major split among First World nations with the following remark:

> We hope that this conference will be an occasion for peoples, through their governments, to call for genuine cultural resistance, a real crusade against this domination, against – let us call a spade a spade – this financial and intellectual imperialism.[19]

The United States reacted to Lang's statement with accusations of chauvinism. There are major problems with a notion of cultural identity as a discrete and super-legitimate phenomenon when this primarily serves as a warrant for an 'asphyxiating localism' created and policed by culture bureaucrats. Its principal effect under such conditions has often been to champion hierarchical and narrow accounts of culture.[20]

Dallas, for example, is routinely held up as an exemplar of 1980s cultural imperialism, notably by Lang himself. One response to its commercial success has been for local producers to model other programmes on it within their own milieux, to render its textual referent local while recycling many of its generic components. This has driven some authorities to very limiting accounts of what may be termed authentic and local. The net effect has been a quaint dynamic of interpenetration and symbiosis between discourses and capital movements under the apparently diffuse signs of globalisation and regionalisation, both dependent on very homogeneous, integrated understandings of culture. There has been a tendency in European debate to conflate 'mass culture' with 'American', denying in the process the extraordinary heterogeneity of the domestic US audience and conflating source of supply with impact at point of consumption.[21]

The reaction of the subordinated cultures is to construct differ-ence and represent it through the concept of nation. But there is little agreement over what nations are, what national identity is, or how to explain national movements, though culture is clearly im-portant at the level of the constitution of community, the perform-ance of 'typical doings and sayings'.[22] A standard language – Pari-sian French – was, for example, an essential component in the emergence of a bourgeoisie after the French Revolution. And when considering what can go into a public's constitution of itself and its surroundings, it is hard to decry facts such as that 87 per cent of English-language Caribbean television was imported in 1988, up 10 per cent in ten years, with most of it in the field of drama.[23]

However, the valorisation of traditional cultural formations is often profoundly repressive of particular categories of person. The enunciation, disposition and protection of a culture may be done by and for local elites in the name of a romanticised harking after authentic community spirit.[24] There is great force behind US Trade representative Carla Hills' uncomfortable question about the EC's TV policy, as to whether 'English culture is promoted more by a film produced in France by "Europeans" than by a film of New Zealand origin.'[25] And away from the attempt to create the alchemical Euro-pean, how plaintively should Jack Lang appeal to national specificity in the language of freedom from media domination when his Minis-try worked strenuously to wrest the balance of TV programming away from the US and Britain via the formation of a Latinate audio-visual locale of France, Iberia and Latin America? It may be that the rhetoric of a single Europe is not much more than an attempt to cut the costs of advertising through standardisation.

Most conceptions of cultural conservation are forwarded by a particular group which claims to possess a particular geopolitical space and to act as guarantor of its cultural validity and authenticity. The dominant definition, for example, of the 'new European' is organised in terms of a Judaeo-Christian set of religious beliefs; Hellenistic accounts of the polity, arts and science; and Roman jurisprudence. European Community directives deploying such logics are increasingly under attack for the partiality of this amal-gam. Critics refer to the EC as 'the official magisters of culture'.[26] When she was Prime Minister of Britain, Margaret Thatcher always insisted that the Community eschew any fantasy of 'some identikit European personality' on the one hand and a Leviathan-like 'super-state' on the other. She was very dubious about an extra-economic component to the Community.

Why is this of such great concern? In 1945, Hans Kohn suggested that, paradoxically, the 'age of nationalism represents the first period of universal history'.[27] What is apparently by definition an enclosure may in fact provide the first prerequisites for internationalism, particularly in terms of the internationalisation of commerce. That process is dependent on formal entities organised around national lines speaking for different peoples, especially in the provision of legal and organisational infrastructures for the accumulation and investment of capital. 'Same' and 'Other' can only be understood individually in relation to their apparent opposite. The nation is best understood as a constantly reformed remaking of tradition and coherence on ever-altered terrain. The original account of the nation as 'a body of people with a common history and descent, a common language, common customs, and a long-standing attachment to a particular piece of ground' is no longer tenable, as J.D.B. Miller points out. The polyethnic nature of most nations now sees them bonded together 'by the fact of the state's existence' and the detritus of the diplomatic cartography of decolonisation.[28] Hence the state's need for vigilance in forming, surveying and reforming cultural subjects. This is especially significant for new polities.

The dominant industrialisation and democratisation logic of the 1960s valorised 'the "free flow of information" principle ... as powerful instruments for achieving the announced goals of socio-economic modernisation, national integration, and cultural expression'.[29] Its proponents were subsequently accused of imposing a Western *telos* on notions of progress/development by misrecognising the political and problematic nature of the nexus between tradition and modernity; applying a transcendentalist social psychology; and neglecting issues of dependency/unequal exchange. Cultural imperialism was regarded as a means of eliciting consent to economic domination from outside, not least through the formation of endemic consumption via advertising.[30]

In turn, however, the functionalist and statist underpinnings of dependency theory were brought into question for their failure to account adequately for factors outside the sovereign-state and inside national boundaries (viz., respectively, the operation of effectively undomiciled multinational corporate capital and the emergence of bourgeoisies within developing countries). World systems theorists would assert that class formation is not necessarily to be found at the site of production, but rather in relation to core-periphery connections, specifically the multifarious locations of different aspects of the delivery of services.[31]

The 1950s and 1960s logic of aid rested on the presumption that the media were a means of dispensing knowledge – the West's owned object – to those less fortunate. This applied equally at the levels of the development of the polity, the economy and what was called the 'modernised individual'. Throughout those decades, the US and UNESCO promulgated research paradigms which directed less developed countries to reinvent themselves in the image of the First World. That process can be contrasted with statements made two decades later by Josh Elbaum, then a sales representative with the US overseas distributor Telepictures, about exports to the Soviet Union: 'Knowing their political sensitivities and constraints we gave them a catalogue that took these sensitivities into account.' He went on to explain that: 'The hardest things to sell in the Caribbean are music specials, because music is a very strong component of their own culture. Even a Bette Midler special with computer enhancement – you couldn't give it away there.'[32] This demonstrates a fully achieved business sense of the need to blend international sales with import cultures' own patterns. The centre now understands, with Elbaum, that shifts in the global political economy require a de-domiciling of corporate thought and planning to include local cultural contours as one more configuration to be parcelled as a 'market niche'.

Along with the boom in services which it was created to manage and alter, the NWICO paradigm has had real effects. It has encouraged a discursive and marketing streamlining that acknowledges the senses of self expressed and determined in the world according to the 'Other'. Sony's in-house term for this is the splendid oxymoron, 'global localisation':

The aim is to be present in many local (or national) markets simultaneously, with the aim of reaping global economies of scale in distributing products across different markets and different media. The challenges facing global companies are to transcend, on the one hand, vestigial national differences in order to create standardised global markets, but also to be sensitive to the peculiarities of local markets and differentiated consumer segments.[33]

This is not uncontested terrain, however, and this counter-counterpower in turn elicits responses, such as parodic local production that offers a sardonic critique of its own status as an import culture.[34] To position the South as hopelessly weak in the field of culture is also to ignore the tremendous contribution to balance of payments figures that exports from, say, the Indian screen make to its economy. And it is worth noting that the fifth biggest US TV chain is the Spanish International Network. Owned by a Mexican, it feeds more than three hundred stations with Mexican, Brazilian and Argentinian drama, reaching between six and ten million viewers. By the end of 1990, just three of Hollywood's seven biggest studios were owned by American capital. There even emerged a critique of foreign control of American business on the grounds that 'self-determination is the solid core of citizenship motivation'.[35] Internationalism was becoming a keyword, a keyword both of opportunity and constraint.

The Global Economy and Cultural Theory

Immanuel Wallerstein has argued persuasively for the globally determined nature of business, in particular the understanding that, regardless of the economic and political formations internal to sovereign-states, if they trade they are part of a capitalist sphere. In his reading, capitalist production is seen to move through various processes. Initially, goods of a certain type are produced and consumed in the centre by one of the international market economy countries. The next phase sees these goods produced there and exported to peripheral economic points. The cycle concludes with production moving to that periphery once technology is sufficiently standardised and labour has the right mix of docility and skill.

In response to accusations of economic determinism and the exclusion of categories of person and practice eluding this approach (categories such as women, ethnic minorities and various forms of cultural distinctness), Wallerstein has latterly considered other areas. He suggests that two critical and distinct definitions of culture have centred nineteenth- and twentieth-century Western debates. These are firstly, 'the set of characteristics which distinguish one group from another'; and secondly, 'some set of phenomena which are different from (and "higher" than) some other set of phenomena within any one group'. The key element mobilised in the process of difference described in the first system is a means of self-formation that permits a recognition of relative sameness in some but not others: 'some kind of self-awareness (and therefore a sense of boundaries)'. The first system sees culture signifying a field of constancy in a space that is actually undergoing, necessarily, constant reinvention because of the dynamic of growth and newness that emblematises capitalism. The second system is invoked to justify inequalities emerging from this process. The valorisation of modernity in the West, Wallerstein maintains, has amounted to a unity between the West's own view of itself and modernity; they become indistinguishable one from the other. Those entities that fail to thrive are held to have mistakenly followed the hermetic conservation precepts of the first system instead of the competitive ethos of the second system.[36]

This binary opposition regards cultural maintenance under the sign of relativism or charity as a form of retardation. Attention to the 'rights' of minorities or formations of persons which are not culturally strong in the face of globalisation, or nationalism, or masculinity, is regarded as an act of economically irrational folly.

Wallerstein may be right about certain aspects of the impulse towards hierarchisation in culture, but he seems to make the discourses of modernisation and rationalisation applied to economies and polities into the masters of modernity. In doing so, he overrides a significant autonomy and reciprocity across these domains. It is a commonplace of the Enlightenment and modernity to fetishise representation because of the complex interrelationship which it is held to have with reading protocols and the structure and operation of the public sphere, in such a way that a cultural openness and relativism are regarded as integral components of the resulting discourse of liberalism.[37] This has become a heterogeneous and confused process which is much less totalising than Wallerstein's account allows.

There has also been a significant impact on the politics of subjectivity deriving from the confluence of an expansion in trade and relocation of production (to the point where distribution is now a critical site). It is a process in which capital formation, state-corporate relations and dispensations towards ethnicity are constitutive of TIS rather than supplementary to it. As a consequence of the world's greatest industrial force trimming itself towards services because of its comparative advantage in the area, there has developed what Jonathan Friedman has called the 'intensive practice of identity . . . this desperate negotiation of selfhood'.[38]

It is assuredly true that daily life is increasingly determined in places and time zones far distant from it. We can all acknowledge the timelessness, placelessness and permissiveness of multinational corporations and their awkward meetings with local cultural norms that are precisely historical, geographical and indigenous, at least rhetorically. This has, though, been seen by some as a fairly straightforward search for a *lingua franca* of the commodity, not a new world citizen. Yet this account too has been found wanting by the sacerdotal celebrants of subcultural resistance. They might not wish to travel the distance with the 'one world culture' position, but they deny the view that cosmopolitanism is always and everywhere imperialising. The new form of image-tourist may be anybody with access to a television service, the immediate audience to dynamic shifts in the world order.

Rupert Murdoch is not alone in rendering paradigmatic the terms 'nation' and 'information', as in his celebrated suggestion that Adam

Smith writing two hundred years on would have retitled his *ur*-text, *The Wealth of Information*.[39] It is clear that the terms of the debate on the traded moving image must now consider a cry to address (which is to form) particular subjectivities. Utopias have shifted from the domain of free labour and free will to free communication.[40]

Notes

1. Richard A. Higgot and Andrew Fenton Cooper, 'Middle Power Leadership and Coalition Building: Australia, the Cairns Group and the Uruguay Round of Trade Negotiations', *International Organization*, vol. 44 no. 4, 1990, pp. 590–4. See also J.G. Starke, *Introduction to International Law*, 10th ed. (London: Butterworth, 1989), p. 386.
2. Stephen Resnick and Richard Wolff, 'Radical Differences Among Radical Theories', *Review of Radical Political Economics*, vol. 20 nos. 2–3, 1988, p. 1.
3. Sandra Braman, 'Trade and Information Policy', *Media, Culture and Society*, vol. 12 no. 3, 1990, pp. 362 and 365. See also Sylvia Ostry, 'New Developments in Trade Policy', *Queen's Quarterly*, vol. 97 no. 2, 1990, pp. 216–17.
4. Colin Hoskins *et al.*, 'US Television Programs in the International Market: Unfair Pricing?', *Journal of Communication*, vol. 39 no. 2, 1989, p. 57; 'Europe's "TV without Frontiers" Missteps at Final Hurdle', *Broadcasting Abroad*, July 1989, p. 6.
5. Peter Brimelow, 'The Dark Side of 1992', *Forbes*, vol. 145 no. 2, 1990, p. 85.
6. 'GATT: Plenty of Talk, Answers yet to Come', *AFC News*, no. 87, 1990, p. 1.
7. Kristin Thompson, *Exporting Entertainment: America in the World Film Market 1907–34* (London: British Film Institute, 1985), pp. 93–9, 114, 117–18 and 121; Thomas Guback, 'Non-Market Factors in the International Distribution of American Films', in Bruce A. Austin (ed.), *Current Research in Film: Audiences, Economics, and Law*, Volume 1 (Norwood: Ablex Publishing Corporation, 1985), p. 123.
8. Tapio Varis, 'Trends in International Television Flow', in Cynthia Schneider and Brian Wallis, *Global Television* (New York: Wedge Press and Cambridge, Mass.: MIT Press, 1988), pp. 97 and 99–101.
9. 'The Entertainment Industry', *The Economist*, vol. 313 nos. 7634–5, 1989, SURVEY 4.
10. Richard Gold, 'Globalization: Gospel for the '90s?', *Variety*, 2 May 1990, p. S–1.
11. Braman, 'Trade and Information Policy', p. 372.
12. A. Frank Reel, *The Networks: How They Stole the Show* (New York: Charles Scribner's Sons, 1979), p. xiii.
13. Janet Staiger and Douglas Gomery, 'The History of World Cinema: Models for Economic Analysis', *Film Reader 4*, 1979, p. 40.

14. Victor de Grazia, 'Mass Culture and Sovereignty: The American Challenge to European Cinemas, 1920–1960', *Journal of Modern History*, vol. 61 no. 1, 1989, p. 53.

15. Quoted in Richard Collins, 'Wall-to-Wall *Dallas*: The US–UK Trade in Television', in Schneider and Wallis, *Global Television*, pp. 79–80.

16. John Tomlinson, *Cultural Imperialism: A Critical Introduction* (London: Pinter Publishers, 1991), pp. 71–2.

17. Steven S. Wildman and Stephen E. Siwek, *International Trade in Films and Television Programs* (Cambridge, Mass.: Ballinger, 1988), p. 150.

18. Industries Assistance Commission, *International Initiatives to Liberalise Trade in Services*, Inquiry into International Trade in Services, Discussion Paper No. 3 (Canberra: Australian Government Publishing Service, 1989), p. 6.

19. Quoted in A. Mattelart *et al.*, 'International Image Markets', in Schneider and Wallis, *Global Television*, pp. 19–20.

20. A. Mattelart *et al.*, 'International Image Markets', pp. 22–3. See also Yi-Fu Tuan, 'Cultural Pluralism and Technology', *The Geographical Review*, vol. 79 no. 3, 1989, p. 270, and Michel Foucault, 'Rituals of Exclusion', in Sylvère Lotringer (ed.), *Foucault Live (Interviews 1966–84)* (New York: Semiotext(e) Foreign Agents Series, 1989), p. 71.

21. Michael Denning, 'The Ends of Ending Mass Culture', *International Labor and Working-Class History*, no. 38, 1990, p. 63; Jean Baudrillard, 'Politics of Seduction', interviewed by Suzanne Moore and Stephen Johnstone, *Marxism Today*, January 1989, p. 54; and Preben Sepstrup, *Transnationalization of Television in Western Europe* (London, Paris and Rome: John Libbey, 1990), pp. 4, 85 and 89.

22. Josep R. Llobrea, 'Nationalism: Some Methodological Issues', *Jaso*, vol. 18 no. 1, 1987, p. 13. See also Ernest Barker, *National Character and the Factors in its Formations* (London: Methuen, 1927), p. 15; Terry Threadgold *et al.* (eds.), *Sydney Studies in Society and Culture*, no. 3 'Semiotics-Ideology-Language', p. 31.

23. 'Isles Full of Foreign Noises', *South*, no. 92, 1988, p. 106.

24. Jeremy Tunstall, *The Media are American: Anglo-American Media in the World* (London: Constable, 1981), p. 58; and Arjun Appadurai, 'Disjuncture and Difference in the Global Cultural Economy', *Theory, Culture & Society*, vol. 7 nos. 2–3, 1990, pp. 295–6.

25. Brimelow, 'The Dark Side of 1992', p. 89.

26. Jan Nederveen Pieterse, 'Fictions of Europe', *Race & Class*, vol. 32 no. 3, 1991, pp. 3, 5 and 6.

27. Hans Kohn, *The Idea of Nationalism: A Study in its Origins and Background* (New York: Macmillan, 1945), p. vii.

28. J. D. B. Miller, 'The Sovereign State and its Future', *International Journal*, vol. 39 no. 2, 1984, p. 284.

29. Chin-Chuan Lee, 'The International Information Order', *Communication Research*, vol. 9 no. 4, 1982, p. 618.

30. Raquel Salinas and Leena Padan, 'Culture in the Process of Dependent Development: Theoretical Perspectives', in Kaarle Nordenstreng and

Herbert Schiller (eds.), *National Sovereignty and International Communication* (New Jersey: Ablex, 1979), pp. 85 and 94.

31. June Nash, 'Ethnographic Aspects of the World Capitalist System', *Annual Review of Anthropology*, no. 10, 1981, p. 396.

32. Quoted in Coco Fusco, 'Telepictures: An Interview with Josh Elbaum', in Schneider and Wallis, *Global Television*, pp. 40 and 43.

33. Asu Aksoy and Kevin Robins, 'Hollywood for the 21st Century: Global Competition for Critical Mass in Image Markets', *Cambridge Journal of Economics*, vol. 16, 1992, p. 18.

34. Ulf Hannerz, 'Culture Between Center and Periphery: Toward a Macro-anthropology', *Ethnos*, vol. 54. nos. 3–4, 1989, p. 213.

35. Marshall Dimock, 'The Restorative Qualities of Citizenship', *Public Administration Review*, vol. 50 no. 1, 1990, p. 22.

36. Immanuel Wallerstein, 'Culture as the Ideological Battleground of the Modern-World System', *Hitotsubashi Journal of Social Studies*, vol. 21 no. 1, 1989.

37. Appadurai, 'Disjuncture and Difference', pp. 299–300.

38. Jonathan Friedman, 'Being in the World: Globalization and Localization', *Theory, Culture & Society*, vol. 7 nos. 2–3, 1990, p. 312.

39. Rupert Murdoch, 'Freedom in Broadcasting', MacTaggart Lecture at the Edinburgh Television Festival, 25 August 1989.

40. Jürgen Habermas, 'The New Obscurity: The Crisis of the Welfare State and the Exhaustion of Utopian Energies', in Shierry Weber Nicholsen (ed.), *The New Conservatism: Cultural Criticism and the Historians' Debate* (Cambridge, Mass.: MIT Press, 1989), pp. 67–8.

Romanian Television:
From Image To History

Pavel Campeanu

For thirty years or more, media researchers have conducted labora-
tory-style experiments to investigate aspects of television communication. In the second half of the 1980s, in a strange quirk of history,
Romania itself was transformed into one such laboratory. A country
of 23 million people was subjected to a communications experiment
which was implemented by the most brutal Stalinist dictatorship in
Eastern Europe as part of a general strategy of repression. I wish to
examine the ways in which the national television monopoly in
Romania was involved in the extraordinary social crisis which led to
revolution. The television service changed in response to the social
crisis, evolving through three distinct stages: before, during and
after the revolution of December 1989. Each of these phases revealed
different relationships between the society in crisis, television programming and/or the television institution, and the audience. I shall
concentrate on the first phase of this evolutionary process and on the
interaction between television programming change and audience
response.

The national domestic crisis deepened rapidly with the decision,
made by the ruling dictator, to repay the country's foreign debt of
more than $12 billion before the end of the decade. Essential and
non-essential goods were harshly restricted: food, heating, electricity
and medical assistance. Laws prohibited domestic use of electrical
installations (with the exception of one light bulb of minimal power
in each room) and the use of private cars on Sundays and during the
winter. Restaurants, theatres and cinemas were not permitted to
open after 9 p.m. People were obliged to spend their evenings at
home, watching television. But very soon this service was also restricted. Under the pretext of saving power, one of the only two TV

channels was suspended, and the remaining channel was reduced from sixty-five to fifteen hours of transmission time per week: two hours for each of the six working days and three hours on Sunday.

In striving to diminish television consumption, the ruling dictatorship had effectively reduced channels for the production and communication of its political ideology. In order to recover part of this loss, the remaining television channel was obliged to restrict the diversity of its output and modify the content. Entertainment, 'real' news, and educational programmes were reduced to a minimal level, while ideology-laden programmes were protected as much as possible. The result was an amazing concentration of ideological messages in the television schedule.

The repercussions and implications of these decisions were extensive, but I shall focus on the reaction of the audience to this attempt to transform the television schedule into a pure instrument of political ideology. The response of the Romanian viewers was a categorical rejection of the new television service. In trying to understand why this was the case I suggest that it is necessary to examine the inherent functions of television communication and consider a number of hypotheses: there is a limited compatibility between the language of television and the specific rhetoric of any ideology; the audience does not reject an excess of ideology as such, but a given ideology of which it disapproves; the audience does not reject in the main the ideological content, but its dislocating effect on programmes dedicated to genuine information and entertainment.

The reorganisation of the content of the television service was a manoeuvre characteristic of a classic monopoly: real demand is not only ignored but met by a supply the market dislikes. In this case the opposition between TV demand and the TV supply imposed by the authorities may be seen as a movement from manipulative to repressive television. This transformation indicates a crucial change in television's previous functions, and takes place at three levels. At the social level, the television schedule is designed entirely to justify a repressive regime, acting as an instrument and a component of a general strategy of repression. At the functional level, while manipulative TV is unobtrusive and based on insinuation, repressive TV is evident and based on coercion. At the operational level, the repressive character of television emerges when its programmes are completely saturated with ideological messages; when the ideology, so transmitted, is brought into disrepute in the eyes of the audience; and when these guiding principles effectively eliminate genuine information and entertainment.

Repression, in this case comparable to the law as a regulator of action, operates by forbidding or imposing certain behaviour. In order to accomplish these ends, both forms of regulation make use of penalties. The law inflicts punishment for crimes, legally defined. In repressive regimes the punishment may be personal or impersonal, related or not to crimes which, if necessary, can be concocted. Television repression, however, does not punish any person and any specific fault. It simply tries, by suppressing any alternative – itself a coercive act – to impose upon the audience defined forms of viewing behaviour. It seeks to ensure audience absorption of TV messages which have been distilled to the essence of the official ideology and which promote the cult of the dictator.

The attempt to regulate, through coercive means, TV viewing behaviour seems highly unusual and ambitious. Such behaviour is naturally protected, on the one hand by its immense territorial dispersion, and on the other by its capacity for concealment. These inherent characteristics, under different political regimes, ensure that watching TV remains an enclave of freedom. The changes to Romanian television programmes, decided upon by the ruling power, tried to demolish this enclave. The response of the Romanian audience was an impulse to defend it.

But how can such an assertion be substantiated when television viewing behaviour is not physically apparent? Audience surveys were no longer permitted in Romania, and therefore nobody could establish to what degree viewers accepted or rejected the new television schedule. The evidence was to be seen from a piece of technical apparatus, a special antenna needed to receive TV programmes from neighbouring countries. Romania has common borders with the Soviet Union to the east, Hungary to the north-west, Yugoslavia to the south-west, and Bulgaria to the south. The technical requirement for obtaining TV reception from these countries was a special antenna which had to be installed on the roof, one for each TV set. With incredible speed, forests of antennae grew on roofs all over the country.

The antennae could be directly observed, but there was other evidence to support the assertion. First, there was a persistent imbalance between demand for and supply of these antennae and this led to substantial price rises. Second, it was difficult to hire specialists to install them, and the charges for this service were exorbitant. Third, the only foreign TV channel available in Bucharest, with a population of nearly three million, was TV Sofia in Bulgaria. The city's university adult education department, where it was possible to take courses of one's choice on payment of fees, faced at that period an unexpected problem. The most popular course was no longer computing, theatre or cosmetics, but Bulgarian, a purely Slavic language, completely different from the Latin Romanian and not a particularly useful international language. For these inhabitants of the Romanian capital, a foreign language was felt to be less alien than the Romanian version of the official propaganda language. Finally, and most significantly, it was interesting to note the remarkable tolerance displayed by the secret police when confronted with these rooftop excrescences. It is important to remember that during the 80s Ceausescu's dictatorship became, fundamentally, a police regime. Using a huge army of informers, the secret police was less secret than its title suggests. Present everywhere, it controlled everything, from the obstetric state of women to the use of typewriters and the repertory of musicians hired to play at private family celebrations. Most people adapted to this exhaustive control by developing a strategy of feigned obedience. But with the antennae on the roofs, pretence was impossible.

The installation of this rooftop apparatus displayed a collective disobedience, a triple defiance of the dictatorship: the rejection of its ideological discourse; the preference for alternative foreign messages; and, in order to reach them, a supplementary consumption of energy, which broke legal restrictions. Confronted with this defiance, the *Securitate* could have reacted with its customary brutality, destroying the installed antennae, forbidding their sale and/or their production. But such 'normal' reactions did not occur. Was this an error, or simply resignation in the face of a *fait accompli*? It was probably both. However, one of the most plausible explanations is that the authorities were too slow to react to the speed and spread of this heretical behaviour and did not understand its real extent.

This is an aspect of a general sociological question about the social effects of technical innovation. Certainly, these poor antennae are not as significant as nuclear power stations, or even TV satellites, but their influence should not be overlooked. The more the antennae proliferated, the less TV viewing behaviour could be preserved as private activity. As a result all pretence of obedient viewing behaviour was unmasked and antennae owners were exposed to the risk of punishment. Implanted not only on rooftops but also in a society affected by a critical domestic crisis, the special antennae assumed a symbolic as well as a direct political significance. Symbolically they denoted audacity and association in disobedience, and politically they signified a transition from hidden to open disobedience. It was this spontaneously co-ordinated resistance which inflicted the first public defeat on the dictatorship, and although apparently insignificant, it was historically productive.

113

To understand the political significance of this act of defiance it is important to emphasise the nature of the Ceausescu regime: it was at that period not only the most anachronistic, but also the most xenophobic form of Stalinism in Europe. Each time a Romanian had contact with foreigners, from the West or the East, it was considered a potential act of espionage. There was a special law which obliged people having such contacts to present a written report to the police within twenty-four hours. Romanians had to be totally isolated from the outside world to make sure they were happy with what they had. However, by using these antennae, they escaped this isolation and established continuous contact with foreign sources which they did not report. They developed, through this mass escape, an alternative mass-media system, in a kind of improvised co-operation with neighbouring countries, and at the same time broke the television state monopoly and xenophobic laws.

In this tense atmosphere it seemed very likely that the police would reverse its policy of non-intervention and take exemplary repressive measures against users of the special antennae. Initial success for users was no guarantee that there would not be future risks. Antennae users had to live with the dangers of an uncertain official response and in so doing they displayed great audacity and collective spirit. The roofs around them were unequivocal proof that people were coming out from their solitude and sharing the danger together. In political terms, it was the first collective, open and successful act of resistance on a national scale in decades. This had great social and political significance. A large section of the population overcame its old, deep reflexes of formal obedience. It broke three orders of the central power: to watch the new, ideology-laden TV programmes; to save energy; and to avoid any contact with foreign countries or persons. The first of these orders was the most important and had a definite purpose: to force the population to assimilate the ideology of its oppressor, the ruling dictatorship. The core of this ideology was the cult of the dictator. The special antennae expressed a disregard for this ideology and for the person who embodied it. Not only did the population not submit to the orders, it acted in a different, if not oppositional way, and by its own initiative. In a society regulated by over-centralised command, individual initiative is regarded as a crime. This is why a collective initiative, clearly directed against the power's will, acquires under these circumstances the features of a quiet rebellion. Taken out of its social context, these claims may seem excessive, but in the case of Romania I would suggest that TV repression incited a TV rebellion.

A particularly exciting aspect of this movement is the nature of the agent of change. Different social groups in different eras have assumed leading roles in phases of social change. In Europe in the first half of this century, this group was for the most part the working class. But in 1968, in Europe and elsewhere, this role was taken on by a completely different group, the student community. In this incident in Romania the group was the TV audience, acting as a community of TV viewers. It was certainly a 'first time' for this community and it might have remained an isolated incident, but today this event is no longer unique: some months ago a similar television crisis occurred in the French island of La Réunion.

This movement, which could be described as a transition from television image to history, occurred in a particular conjuncture of circumstances in Romania: a social environment characterised by crisis; a relatively underdeveloped TV system; a change involving the restriction of TV programming; and an active rejection of this change by the audience. I would suggest that it is precisely by performing this active rejection that the audience transformed itself into what I shall call a viewers' community. The human assembly is the same in both, but its social function is substantially different. In order to change its social function, the audience has to alter its main characteristics, such as the mutual isolation of its members; its passivity in the process of communication (resulting in television's special vulnerability to manipulation); its marginality with respect to political life; and its contribution to the atomisation of the society. To a large extent, these features represent the social and psychological consequences of given technical conditions. The social crisis could not modify these technical conditions, but it could profoundly influence some of the social and psychological effects. Mutual isolation was replaced by synchronised resistance, passivity by action, atomisation by convergence, marginality by visible prominence.

These unspectacular, internal transformations of the TV audience were not without effect on the great event which followed. It is well known that in December 1989 Romanian television played its part in the revolution and, together with TV stations from abroad, transmitted scenes of momentous historical events on live television. Less well known is the fact that television came under attack from counter-revolutionary forces once it had changed its political position. Television then launched an appeal to the audience to rescue the television centre and its staff. Within a few hours the building was surrounded and protected by a huge crowd whose only weapon was its magnitude. Once again, the viewers' community was in action, this time not to resist the dictatorship, but to defend the revolution.

I am not sure this second historic act could have occurred without being preceded by the first anti-dictatorial TV rebellion. There is, between these two moments, continuity and change in the behaviour of the viewers' community. The objective and the form of this action changed, but its new social function persisted: that of an active agent in social and political life, able to play, in certain circumstances, a substantial role.

Television and *Glasnost*: Television and Power*

Sergei Muratov

This year (1991) Soviet Television will be sixty years old; for fifty-five of those years it has been a product of the political administrative system and an instrument of its self-preservation. However, the last five years have seen television developing in conditions of an emerging *glasnost*. For the first time in our country the concepts 'television' and '*glasnost*' have been shown to be compatible and even interdependent.

Experience tells us that modern revolutions begin with the seizure of television and radio, and *perestroika* was no exception. Our country's television was seized by its viewers. This was first evident in the voice of the rebellious 'stairs', the group of teenagers who commandeered the stairs outside the studio of the youth programme *Twelfth Storey*. The stairs were immediately transformed from being merely a location into an expression of audience engagement. Live broadcasting, which has increased twentyfold in the past two years, gave birth to programmes in which there was audience 'contact', giving viewers the right to invade the screen. Television emerged from its lethargy. Some of the best programmes were Vladimir Pozner's *Space Bridges*, Vladimir Molchanov's *Before and after Midnight*, reports from the production team of *View* (which changed from a light entertainment programme to a political discussion programme), the late-night news and the Leningrad channel's *Fifth Wheel* and *Public Opinion*. On screen the heroes of the *nomenklatura*

* This essay was written before the break-up of the former Soviet Union in December 1991. For subsequent events, see 'Afterword: Television in Russia and the CIS since the Coup' at the end of this book (eds.)

were replaced by 'restructured' presenters who advocated *perestroika*. Thanks to the broadcasting of parliament, the people's deputies from Sakharov to Sobchak became national heroes. Television not only showed the mechanism of a restructured society but itself became part of that mechanism. It changed from being a product of *glasnost* to providing the conditions for *glasnost*, conditions that became increasingly decisive.

But this did not suit everyone. The first open confrontation came in March 1988 at the Fourth Plenum of the Film-makers' Union, when there was open condemnation of the television administration's decisions to remove, yet again, TV presenters from programmes and to attempt to retain the right to decide the fate of 'shelved' films. During the plenum the film director E. Ryazanov published an open letter in which he severed ties with the leadership of Gostelradio; soon afterwards, TV presenters Vladimir Tsvetov and Vladimir Pozner moved from the first All-Union channel to the Moscow channel. The following year the idea of decentralisation gripped the country. Siberia and the Far East began to set up their own programmes, bypassing Central Television. Dozens of independent film production associations and hundreds of regional cable TV centres appeared. A number of newspapers and journals began to issue their own video sheets.

In 1990 the process of de-monopolisation turned into open confrontation between the administration and its opponents. The administration made its first attempt to get rid of *View* by cancelling its New Year programme; it closed down the weekly slot *7 Days* just as it was beginning to gain popularity; and dismissed the presenter, Georgy Kuznetsov, from the Moscow channel. On 6 April, deputies from the Leningrad Soviet made a tough decision to 'seize' the city's TV studio and show their programme. The Baltic republics and Moldova announced that they were leaving the Gostelradio system. The phrase 'television and democracy' seemed increasingly to mean 'television or democracy: which will get the upper hand?'

It would be strange if in such circumstances the idea of alternative forms of television did not arise. This idea was first proposed in the June 1988 issue of *Ogonyok* by the TV journalist Vladimir Tsvetov. He wrote that creativity was impossible under ideological control, and that the standardisation of programmes on Central Television did not give viewers the right of choice. The only way out was to set up a parallel form of television. The article started a polemic which continues unabated to this day. As a result, in the public mind, two types of broadcasting have taken shape: alternative television (variously called the 'second one', 'the other', 'independent', 'public', 'the people's'), and state television (termed 'official', 'diplomatic', 'the President's').

With the issue raised in this way, viewers had few doubts about their preferred choice between 'official' and 'public' television. Unfortunately, nobody grasped the meaning of the reaction of the Gostelradio chiefs: they greeted the threat to their broadcasting monopoly almost with enthusiasm. For if alternative television expressed the interests of society, then state programmes were freed from this responsibility.

But there was a more substantial reason. The All-Union channel, the forum with real power, remained in the hands of Gostelradio and its opponents did not aspire to a controlling share of that power. They seemed prepared to be satisfied with regional cable networks and evening programmes and were content to be given Central Television's fourth channel, with its quite localised audience. They did not count on having a more substantial audience for about ten years. I believe that supporters of alternative television let down the very viewers who depended on them in their pursuit of this short-term strategy of setting up independent regional or local networks. However, some believed in a second strategy: reforming Central Television. The conditions seemed right for a 'screen revolution', following on from the newspaper revolution that had taken place in the first years of *glasnost*. For example, the People's Front of Estonia emerged after a discussion on live television.

The euphoria did not last long. A final blow came with the events at the beginning of 1991: the offensively tendentious reporting of the Lithuanian tragedy in January, when thirteen people died after a group from OMON, the special militia detachment, seized the Vilnius TV centre; the dismissal of the late-night news presenters, and the closing down of *View*. Although *View*'s founders continued to make films from their apartments and distributed them on videocassettes, thus realising the idea of alternative television in its pure form, these events put an end to hopes of seeing 'Central Television with a human face'. There was a public outcry. One of the placards at the January 1991 rally in Moscow outside the Kremlin walls read: 'The Goebbels Prize to Central Television's First Channel'. Never before had the press reacted so angrily to the ruthless methods used by the television administration. Unfortunately this criticism focused mainly on the struggle with the chairman of Gostelradio.

The *de facto* head of Gostelradio in the years when the boldest experiments took place on the screen was the same man who is today's chairman. I would suggest that reducing all problems to questions about individual heads is the same as swearing at the thermometer because we don't like the temperature it shows, while the illness turns inwards. The poet Andrey Voznesensky, looking at the Ostankino TV tower, called it 'a syringe for ideological injections', but I would go further in describing All-Union television itself as a kind of enormous syringe: an instrument directed at affecting the audience. But the less it takes account of the opinions of its socially heterogeneous audience, the less the audience takes account of the opinion of television.

Now the reporting of national conflicts quite often sparks off new conflicts. 'Why are all your newsreaders and presenters exclusively Muscovites and Russian?' perplexed foreigners who follow our programmes ask. They are Muscovites because our television is not All-Union but Moscow-based (Central). When, a quarter of a century ago, the Orbita system for the first time brought all Soviet viewers together, it did not change the character of broadcasting: the size of the syringe changed. For decades central administrative snobbery has manifested unconcealed contempt for local studios, whose transmissions to an All-Union audience were permitted only in the form of ostentatious reports and greetings. The centre was concerned not so much to co-ordinate regional channels as to subordinate them. These actions of Central Television bluntly demonstrate its return to the era when programmes were more like crosswords with the letters already filled in.

The 1990 Presidential Decree on the democratisation of television did not ease the situation. On the one hand the decree stated that the legal status of television had to be reviewed; that monopoly of broadcasting by one party was not permitted; and that every public movement had a right to airtime; but on the other hand, the same document announced that Gostelradio's property and facilities were sacrosanct. This last declaration reminds us of the experience of our newspapers where the real power resided with those in charge of the printing press and the paper. Who then is the 'owner' of the airwaves? It is likely to be those who control the transmitters, the TV studios and satellite links. So what was the principal message of the Presidential Decree, that our television had to change or that it was impossible to change it? Strangely, the decree seemed to be saying both, reflecting the real contradictions between the traditions of authoritarian television and the emerging democracy. In a sense it was this contradiction that made the document worthwhile, because it provided an opportunity for discussion of future television law.

But public discussion did not really take place, although television journalists and Russia's Ministers responsible for Justice and for the Mass Media have responded to the decree. It has been much simpler to condemn the moral qualities of the chairman or to boycott television, as the Union of Film-makers did, thus adding to the list of those dismissed by the administration, and the even longer list of those who have left of their own accord. But the strength of a system is not in its people but in its structure, which either includes or does not include a mechanism which allows society to influence the content of programmes. In this sense one can say that the present [1991] system recruits the people it needs. There can be no success in attempts to reform Central Television without radical changes to its structure. Not because television belongs to the state, but precisely because it does not.

The idea that we do not have state broadcasting was first expressed by Eduard Sagalayev in *Izvestiya* more than a year ago. It is noteworthy that on the day the article came out the so-called seizure of Leningrad television took place. Many have written that this action was illegal and, in general, they are correct. But let us examine this incident. Leningrad television was not seized by a group from the special militia detachment, OMON, but by people's deputies, appropriate representatives of the state at the municipal level. If representatives of the state are forced to 'seize' a studio to demonstrate their legal right to be heard, the question arises: from whom, strictly speaking, do they have to win this right? If we do not have state or All-Union broadcasting, then we have to return to the question: who in our country determines broadcasting policy? Is it the USSR Supreme Soviet? If so, why then was the Supreme Soviet's decision to show videos of the tragic events in Tbilisi and in Vilnius to an All-Union audience ignored by the leadership of Central Television?

Recently, we hear increasingly that broadcasting policy is conducted on behalf of the President [i.e. Gorbachev]. Obviously the President has more right than anyone else to have his views aired. But what does 'more' mean? Are we talking of a special slot, or a separate channel, or do we mean all four channels of Central Television, including the Leningrad channel which most Muscovites receive? And if we say 'more than anyone else', then what airtime do these 'others' have the right to hope for? It is these questions of political status that should be regulated by television law, after nationwide discussion and adoption by the Union parliament. The Law on the Press and other Mass Media is not, for instance, considered relevant to television by the leadership of Gostelradio (recently renamed the All-Union State TV and Radio Broadcasting Company), and the authors of this legislation did not include the specificity of broadcasting in their provisions. As a result, the President's television is a 'moratorium on information' or a 'curfew of the air'.

But does a state that wants television broadcasting to be based on the principles of law need public television? Different countries have found different ways of establishing state broadcasting to express the interests of its citizens: the Governors and consultative committees of the BBC; a parliamentary commission which approves the composition of the administrative council in Italy; broadcasting associations in Holland. There is nothing similar in the structure of Soviet broadcasting. It is no coincidence that many people call our television the most lawless in the world.

When the Lithuanian parliament declared its independence, the first thing it did was to switch off the Leningrad channel after *Fifth Wheel* had shown a rally of opponents of 'Sajudis'. The next thing Lithuanian television did was to deprive its political opponents of the possibility of putting forward their views on the air. Obviously this does not justify the invasion by the OMON, but it undoubtedly testifies to the violation of the principle of equal rights for all citizens. Democracy, after all, commits not only its opponents but also its supporters to display tolerance.

It is said that there is no such thing as independent television. This is true: all television is dependent, including ours. The question is on whom does it depend: on the system of the rule of the *nomenklatura* and a Party now in its death throes, or on a society which has for the first time realised its strength? In the first case the most popular programmes and presenters can be taken off with impunity and without consultation with the viewers. In the second, respect is shown for the viewers and this is the basis of programming policy.

'Television moulds citizens and makes them easy to govern.' In the first years of *glasnost* this comment by a French political scientist could be disputed. The 'people's journalism' on the screen and the transmission of parliament showed that television could also inform citizens who themselves were learning to govern. State broadcasting which answers and expresses the interests of the audience is alternative television; it does not exclude other kinds of alternative broadcasting, and it effectively opposes the form of television run by the Party apparatus and the Party *nomenklatura*.

The main success of the *perestroika* years does not lie in the new programmes which, as we have seen, can be re-edited or removed, or even in the new presenters, who can be dismissed. Its success lies in the changing consciousness of an enormous section of the audience: the new viewer who has felt for the first time that he is perhaps not

122

simply an object but the subject of broadcasting. Such viewers cannot be removed or dismissed. They already sense that television should speak not only on behalf of those in power, but on behalf of those who delegate that power.

News on Soviet Television: Breakthrough to Independence

Eduard Sagalayev

A British journalist once told me: 'In Britain we have many demo-cratic institutions: parliament, the courts, the rights of the individ-ual, and media freedom. But the British would be prepared to give up all of them except media freedom, because with that we could immediately regain all the other democratic institutions.' Media freedom is the vertebra that enables us to restore the whole skeleton. Media freedom is the key to democracy.

In our country we have virtually never had media freedom. Nor do we have it now. *Glasnost* today is free speech in doses. The amount of freedom can increase or decrease depending on the politi-cal situation and the dose is determined, as before, by the Party and government apparatus. Everything we say and write we do, not because we are free, but because we have been given permission. We remain an extremely controlled society. Television mirrors the state of society and cannot be better or worse than the policies it serves.

During the period of stagnation, television was required to create an image of prosperity and abundance: rich ears of corn filled the screens, combine harvesters rolled off conveyor belts, new housing estates grew like mushrooms, more and more railway lines ran into the distance, and gazing out at us from the television screen were the happy, contented faces of Soviet people, owners of this fantastic world. Obviously it was not all untrue; it had a measure of truth, but the positive images had been painstakingly assembled.

Does television mirror life? Yes, but television has always been a magic mirror, rather like the one used by the foolish Empress in the fairy tale by the poet Aleksandr Pushkin. It is one such mirror that Soviet people have been forced to look at. It carefully concealed and smoothed out the ugliness and imperfections of life; it was hypnotic and consoling and, despite all evidence to the contrary, asserted in visual images: 'You, the country of triumphant socialism, are beautiful. You are dearer than any other on earth!' Then came other times and other leaders, and television also changed. As the shoots of democracy burst forth, so they did on the screen: in live broadcasts, on TV debates during pre-electoral campaigns, and in the transmission of parliamentary sessions and congresses. As far as it was allowed, television reflected a country preoccupied with new political ideas, and for a short period it became a real mirror of life; as contradictory as life itself and therefore a little more accurate.

In 1988, I was appointed head of the News Service on Soviet television. The only news programme in the Soviet Union, *Vremya* (*Time*), had been transmitted every day for twenty years and during that period its concept of news had not changed one iota. Paradoxically, *Vremya* had never been a news programme in the generally accepted sense of the word. It informed viewers, not of what was happening in the country and in the world, but of what our Party leaders wanted to see. News was not concerned with information but with propaganda and counter-propaganda. Thus in the course of two decades it never reported the catastrophes or national disasters which occurred in our country from time to time; whereas such news from abroad filled our screens to such an extent that viewers must have had the impression that any day the capitalist world would go up in flames.

Being a romantic by nature and believing that any change I might make would be irreversible, I assumed that I would be able to change news policy on Soviet television. I managed to reduce radically the amount of so-called 'protocol', the reading of Party documents by the newsreader in close-up. I brought in young talented journalists who were not weighed down by stereotypical ideological thought. Until then those working on the programme had mainly been veterans of our patriotic school of TV journalism, who had asserted many times over their political loyalty. I brought in journalist-commentators to present the news, rather than just newsreaders who read texts written by others.

Nevertheless, I was not allowed to change news policy substantially. I was constantly under pressure and the watchful control of the Party and government apparatus. Understandably, a party intent on preserving the system was not going to let such a powerful institution as television slip through its fingers. At that time I dreamt of filming a short report from my office. I would explain to the viewers, who were making increasing complaints about the content of our news, how it was done. For ninety per cent of my time I was forced to answer incoming phone calls on a special telephone line: the Kremlin telephone exchange used by top Soviet Party and state bureaucrats. Practically no one really interested in the fate of the country or the people ever rang me. Most of my callers were interested either in covering up some information or getting some self-advertisement, demanding that some state function, highly insignificant in the scale of things, be covered by *Vremya*, the country's leading programme. I would refuse, but later I would be instructed by my bosses to do so. This is in itself unnatural: it is the editor who should decide what to show and what to say. But our system is based on telephone instructions and half of what appears on *Vremya* is decided by these phone calls. Our hands are tied and we are forced to spend money, energy and priceless airtime on rubbish.

In such a situation it is ridiculous to talk of the objectivity and independence of the news. Any objectivity is weighed against Party and other corporate interests. Sometimes this is reduced to absurdity. During the events in the Baltics in January 1991 when the whole world, holding its breath, watched as Soviet tanks crushed *perestroika* with their tracks, *Vremya* began one of its programmes with a report on the 'main' event of the day, the laying of wreaths to Lenin at the Mausoleum. And only towards the end of the news, in passing and briefly, did it report the armed confrontation in Latvia.

To make a news programme without news is a special art. In April 1989, after the tragedy in Tbilisi, we were forbidden to report that spades (specially designed to dig trenches) had been used as weapons against the people. 'This is not a proven fact,' we were told. We objected, saying that as there were witnesses at the scene, we should report it. In reply we were told, 'And what if there were no spades? By reporting this you will have undermined confidence in the Centre and assisted in the disintegration of the country.' As a result we put out 'reports' of this kind: 'Tbilisi, 11 April. The shops are open, people are walking in the streets, the mood is not cheerful, children are at school, there is military hardware on the streets.' The journalist who wrote this report was not lying: people were walking in the streets, but we were silent about the reasons for the tragedy, about the use of tear gas and spades as weapons, about the number of people killed. After the airing of such 'objective' reports crowds gathered on the streets of Tbilisi, chanting: 'Shame on Central Television! Shame on *Vremya*!' Later, on different occasions, similar crowds and similar slogans appeared on the streets of Vilnius and Riga, Erevan and Baku, Dushanbe and Osha.

And yet in that period we were able, if only for a short time as we were to find out later, to make a breakthrough in independent, objective news reporting. Realising that we would never be allowed to change *Vremya*, a group of young journalists and I decided to set up an alternative news programme. This is how *TSN (Television News Service)* was born. It attempted as much as possible to assuage the hunger for news felt by Soviet TV viewers. From the very beginning *TSN* modelled itself on the best overseas news programmes. It did not report the everyday round of Party and government events; it completely ignored the enormous number of official visits and unimportant meetings; it avoided reports on the laying of wreaths at the countless monuments to the founder of the Soviet state and the leader of the Bolsheviks; it omitted news from the fields and factories. Instead *TSN* reporters gave up-to-date and on-the-spot reports of the most important events in the country. The programme substantially changed the view of priorities in news and politics. For example, in November 1990 the national conflicts in the republic of Moldova coincided with the visit of the USSR President, Gorbachev, to Spain. *Vremya* began its news with a report of the visit. *TSN* began with news from Moldova since, however important Gorbachev's visit was from the point of view of foreign policy, our people at the time were more worried about what was happening in Moldova. *TSN* widened as much as possible its sources of information. If *Vremya* chiefly relied on Tass for its reports, *TSN* made use of information from overseas agencies and from a series of newly established independent news agencies in our country.

From *Vremya* viewers learnt something or other about something or other; from *TSN* they learnt what was most important about the most important. The initial coexistence of two such different programmes within the framework of one editorial department of Central Television can be explained in two ways. *Vremya* was considered to be the source of official news; everything else was secondary and not worthy of attention. The second explanation is amusing: as *TSN* came on the air after midnight, top state functionaries simply did not watch it. How else can one explain what, in an authoritarian system, is an incomprehensible fact: that throughout *TSN*'s first year it was able to do whatever it liked with virtually no censorship or any important guiding instructions from the Central Committee, the Council of Ministers or the Supreme Soviet? God and conscience guided the programme-makers, safeguarding them from lies and opportunism. It was not surprising that *TSN*'s rating grew steadily and it soon became the most popular news programme among broad sections of the population.

However, the January 1991 events in the Baltics led to a sharp confrontation between the two programmes. *Vremya* and *TSN* became antagonists in their news coverage. *TSN* would factually contradict information that a few hours earlier *Vremya* had transmitted. Thus *Vremya* reported that the situation in Vilnius was calm and that there was no military presence, while *TSN* showed tanks and the first people to be killed and wounded. It was then that highly placed functionaries from the Central Committee of the Communist Party decided to make up for their laxity and put an end to the breeding ground for rebellion within Central Television. *TSN*'s presenters were forbidden to give their own commentaries and were advised to read out Tass reports instead. *Vremya* by that time had become a direct conduit for information from Tass. It was at this point that political censorship was revived and repeatedly reinforced, acts which were in violation of Article 1 of the Media Law, which states: 'The press and other mass media are free. Censorship of the mass media is not permitted.' Soon afterwards the presenters on *TSN* were sacked and the programme became an appendage of *Vremya*, which was hosted by journalists who had been screened for their political loyalty and lack of civic principle.

An earlier attempt to produce a news programme, *7 Days*, as an alternative to *Vremya* had also come to a sad end after only five months. *7 Days* was transmitted on Sundays, and replaced *Vremya*. It summarised the news of the week, showing and analysing the main domestic and world events. This summary of events, as I now realise, was not in the best interests of the country's leaders. It was one thing to show a number of the day's events on *Vremya*, making certain that there was a balance between tragic items and optimistic ones. It was another matter when viewers were shown the events of the week in a concentrated form. It became obvious, then, that the dramatic and tragic events in our society far outweighed the happy, optimistic ones which the country's leadership wanted to see. This was one reason why the programme was closed down. The second reason, in my view, was that it did not suit the country's leaders to have the week's events summed up by journalists rather than by the Party and government. I presented *7 Days* with the well-known journalist Aleksandr Tikhomirov. The first move came against Tikhomirov, who was dismissed because the authorities did not like his sharp commentaries on the national conflicts in the Caucasus, his evaluation of the economic situation in the country or his forecasts for the future.

Soon after this, at a session of the Politburo of the Central Committee, a special discussion of *7 Days* was included on the agenda. The Politburo's resolution recommended that Gostelradio restore

128

Vremya to its Sunday slot. The Politburo's 'recommendation', though technically illegal since Article 6 of the Constitution had by then been abolished, was put into effect by the chairman of Gostelradio, Mikhail Nenashev, who was also a member of the Communist Party Central Committee. According to established tradition, heads of Soviet television have always been members of the Communist Party Central Committee and are therefore under strict obligation to maintain Party discipline. The programme was stopped, demonstrating that the abolition of Article 6 was no more than a formality. Power has remained in the same hands and television first and foremost still serves those in power. The people have no influence on their television service, although it is 'they' who fund it through taxes. Although our state today is no longer totalitarian, it retains an authoritarian power structure. And in the final analysis the state and its television are governed by a narrow band of people who have power over everything.

The closure of *7 Days* was a glaring example for me and for millions of people that real power in the country remained, as before, in the hands of the top echelon of the Party and the apparatus which served its interests. It was then that I came to the conclusion that it was necessary to set up independent television. Establishing alternative public television would bring about competition; air different views of what was happening in the country; destroy All-Union TV; and give a vigorous impetus to the development of television as a whole, including state television, which had been dragging out its miserable puppet-like existence.

In principle, the rise of the Russian Republic's sovereignty, with the oppositionist Boris Yeltsin heading the republic as well as Russian republican TV, has led to the break-up of All-Union Television's monopoly. It has not, in my opinion, brought us closer to forming independent, public TV. Editors of the Russian TV's news programme *Vesti* (*News*) intended it to be modern in form and content, a programme to be respected, not politically biased in its news coverage but giving the fullest possible picture of events of political significance in the world. Unfortunately Russian TV, in practice, also fulfils certain political objectives and serves the interests of a certain political force. Therefore the independence of the news programme in the Russian republic is relative. So from *Vremya* and the 'modified' *TSN* we get the views of the USSR Supreme Soviet and the Communist Party Central Committee, and from *Vesti* we get the views of the Russian Republic's Supreme Soviet and the Democratic Russia party. What can an ordinary person do if he simply wants to know what is really happening? He is tired of picking up grains of objective information here and there; and he does not trust deputies from the different parliaments, because he can see daily how they struggle for power and play different political cards, using whatever means possible.

The point of independent people's television is to try to be as independent as possible. I envisage such television as a channel, paid for by subscribers, founded by a group of public organisations and private individuals who will become co-owners in a shareholding. This channel would give viewers an objective picture of events, and compare different views of an event. It would try to present a real plurality of opinion. The independent mass media could play a very significant role in developing the beginnings of democracy in our society. State television, whether it be All-Union or All-Russian, cannot by definition be independent. In fact, many talented journalists who have left Central Television have not transferred to the newly established Russian Television in order to avoid being dependent, once again, on another political state structure.

I took part in the first attempt to set up an independent channel while I was still working at Central Television. In the autumn of 1990 I left the News Service convinced that politics is a dirty business and having realised that I no longer wanted to participate actively in it. I began setting up an independent television channel called *TV – 21st Century*. Many of my colleagues reproached me for opting out of the struggle at such an intensely difficult time. But I felt that I had to adopt a radical position to lead us out of the moral and political morass in which we found ourselves. I conceived of my channel as a moral-educational one, capable of rearing the generation of the next century and of objectively informing people of what is happening in this country and the world.

Unfortunately, the best intentions are undermined not only by political resistance but by our poverty in elementary technology. I had to begin from scratch. I negotiated with organisations and people willing to become the founders and shareholders of the channel. I was certain that despite many obstacles and difficulties I could set up this channel. However, at the end of 1990, television took a drastic step backwards: the most controversial and popular programmes were shut down and the most talented and courageous journalists were banned or dismissed. Television set out, as before, to comfort, entertain and distract Soviet viewers from urgent problems on the grounds that truth was bringing about the disintegration of the country and the nation. I am convinced that showing the *corps de ballet* on the screen is blasphemous when your country is counting up the number of people killed and lamenting their fate. The decision was cynical, morally ruinous and, most important, it assisted in the collapse and disintegration of the country.

I realised that I could no longer serve this unprincipled decision; I could no longer fit in with this return to old policies, I could not bow to or fulfil instructions. The people who govern television today do not seem to be aware that they are doomed to political and creative death: a short time will pass, the political climate will change and they will be thrown overboard. As for me, I believe that if there is any real possibility of defending television and preserving *glasnost*, then it is only an independent organisation that can resist the threat of reaction. For this reason I agreed to become the leader of the USSR Union of Journalists, which could become just such a force.

In addition, I am head of the Association of Cable and Broadcasting Television, which consists of more than thirty private and co-operative TV studios and networks, numbering from 2,000 to 200,000 viewers and operating in different cities throughout the country. With like-minded people, I am working to set up a commercial joint stock TV company. But this is in the future – we have only started on the road to genuine independence.

Afterword:
Television in Russia
and the CIS since the Coup

Daphne Skillen

The fate of television in what is now the former Soviet Union is as unpredictable as that of the geo-political space in which it operates. The essays on Soviet television in this collection were written just a few months before the abortive coup of August 1991. Since then we have witnessed the end of seventy-four years of Communist rule, the disintegration of the Soviet empire and the ousting of Gorbachev. Television has entered a new political era.

These essays, however, point to a crucial stage in the struggle for media independence, written as they were at a rather bleak period when renewed censorship and harsh policies were being implemented under Gorbachev's alliance with the hardline leaders, who later tried to depose him. The chairman of All-Union Television, Leonid Kravchenko, appointed in November 1990, had turned the first channel into a mouthpiece for these hardline views. Opposition came from Yeltsin's Russian TV, the second nationwide channel, but it was badly funded and Kravchenko's company, which wielded real power, had allotted it only six hours of airtime a day. Liberal programme-makers increasingly realised that the only way to avoid the arbitrary misuse of state television and the swings of the political pendulum was to campaign for an independent sector which would guarantee them a voice and accommodate those who had been sacked by Kravchenko or had left in protest. The principles of independent programming which were laid down at this time have formed the basis of changes taking place in television today. The development of the independent sector was instrumental, as well, in the successful defeat of the coup.

In the nature of attempted coups, the first step on the conspirators' agenda was to send tanks to surround the Ostankino TV Centre in Moscow, while inside the building armed soldiers patrolled the corridors. Kravchenko had been briefed earlier and reports of the take-over by the State Emergency Committee and Gorbachev's alleged illness were broadcast over the first channel throughout the coup. Russian TV and other channels in Moscow were closed down. So were all but nine newspapers. By bringing troops and tanks into Moscow the plotters believed the old reflex of fear would keep the public off the streets. But just as they misjudged the real changes that had taken place in Soviet society, so they did not fully comprehend that the old monopolistic stranglehold over television had considerably loosened.

While their colleagues at TV Centre were restricted in their movements, journalists in the independent sector got to work. Because of the clampdown on television over the past year, many of the most controversial TV presenters had formed their own independent companies and had their own equipment. Moreover, six years of *perestroika*, with its ups and downs, had produced a large corps of journalists and programme-makers experienced in the struggle for democratic reform. Aleksandr Lyubimov, the TV host of the popular programme *View*, which had also gone independent, points out that his moment of truth came not with the coup but much earlier in 1987 when he had had to battle constantly against pressure to muzzle the programme. For such well-known campaigning journalists, fighting the coup was not heroics, he told me, but simply a matter of survival.

The independent *View* defied the state of emergency by sending out its camera crews to cover the events taking place in the streets, as did Russian TV and other independent companies. Journalists of all branches of the medium used whatever outlets they could find to disseminate resistance: they produced a 'Common Paper', made use of breaches in the TV and radio ban in different parts of the country, and worked with foreign correspondents. Within the TV Centre itself it was reasonably quiet, but there was enough resistance to crack the plotters' facade of invincibility. One of the most striking images that remains of the coup is of the uncontrollably shaking hands of Gennadi Yanayev, the man assuming Gorbachev's duties, filmed at the Emergency Committee's press conference. The editor had refused to obey orders to edit out the shot.

The official news programme *Vremya* did more than dent the plotters' image. In the nine o'clock news the news team managed, because the relevant people chose to look the other way, to show a video report of the barricades and crowds outside Yeltsin's headquarters in the White House. By this device the whole country was informed that Yeltsin was heading the opposition from the White House and Muscovites, in particular, therefore knew precisely where to go if they wanted to oppose the coup.

Immediately after the coup, Kravchenko was sacked and replaced by Yegor Yakovlev, former editor of the newspaper *Moscow News*. This was a political appointment as Yakovlev had spent most of his working life in the print medium. The first thing he did was to sack members of the KGB – the so-called part-timers on the television staff who were living off the company's payroll. Yakovlev appointed Eduard Sagalayev his second in command, in charge of television programming.

The demise of the Soviet Union brought an end to Soviet television. Under a decree signed by Yeltsin on 27 December 1991, the new Ostankino Russian State Television and Radio Company was formed. Running parallel with it is Russian TV, which has taken over the whole second channel. Ostankino TV has inherited the mantle of the former All-Union first channel, except that its brief now is to serve the Commonwealth of Independent States. It has abandoned the term Central TV, with its connotations of Moscow domination, for Inter-State. As with many organisations since the break-up of the Soviet Union, Ostankino TV is in a period of transition, and how it will look when it emerges is not yet clear. Its avowed aim, however, is to set up joint programme-making with the national TV studios of the CIS member states, exchanging information with them on politics, economics and culture.

Although the response from the CIS member states to the new Inter-State channel has been quite positive, in practice their behaviour has been erratic. Moldova has cut off Ostankino TV's broadcasts for long periods, provoking the ire of the Russian-speaking population. Ukraine has agreed to transmit the two Russian channels but it has switched over its powerful transmitters, once used for the All-Union channel, to transmit its own Ukrainian channel. Other former republics have dropped Ostankino's programmes when it has suited them. There is undisguised suspicion of what some still regard as Ostankino TV's imperialist ambitions and, admittedly, Ostankino TV is Russian; on the other hand the financial burden at present is wholly shouldered by the Russian state budget.

Given this situation Yegor Yakovlev, in an open letter addressed to leaders of the CIS, published in *Izvestiya* on 4 March 1992, has proposed turning Ostankino TV into the International Broadcasting Company, in which the founding members of the company will be the CIS member states. Financing will be shared out according to the population figures and transmission costs of each independent state. A representative Supervisory Council will resolve 'frequent inaccuracies and occasional bias' in news coverage. Yakovlev's proposal has been accepted in principle, but national and political disagreements prevail. As the representative from Moldova bluntly pointed out at one meeting: 'Why should we receive and pay for programmes with undesirable information?' Indeed, it is unclear how the Supervisory Council will manage to reach any compromise between, say, the Armenian and Azerbaidzhani representatives over news coverage of Nagorno Karabakh, or between any of the sides engaged in national and ethnic disputes. But these problems do not invalidate the advantages of maintaining ties, through television, with diverse nationalities that were once considered 'united and indivisible'.

This is apparently what television viewers want. In a March 1992 *Izvestiya* opinion poll conducted in the capital cities of eight former republics, in which about 7,000 people were questioned, the results showed that the majority of people regularly watched Ostankino TV: moreover, in seven out of eight cases the indigenous non-Russian population preferred to watch Ostankino TV rather than their own republican television. It appears that while leaders wrangle over political questions, ordinary viewers not only wish to preserve a familiar staple of their lives but probably appreciate the inevitably greater professionalism of former Central TV.

The reorganisation of Ostankino TV, then, has not been finalised but changes within the company have already taken place. The entire staff of the former Gostelradio have been sacked and contracts negotiated with individuals and independent companies. Proposals for financing television either through a licence fee or advertising are being considered. Television has been warned that it has less than a year to map out its future as Russia's dwindling state budget will no longer be able to subsidise it. Plans for setting up a separate non-state channel are not considered by those working in television to be as much of a priority at present as dismantling and taking a piece of the pie that was the most powerful propaganda medium in the Soviet Union. What happens to Ostankino TV will determine the fate of television generally.

We have yet to see if the new leaders in Russia will encroach upon the newly acquired media freedoms. Certainly Yeltsin has for a long time been committed to media pluralism, and his recent decrees and some of his actions – such as stepping in to resolve a conflict in favour of St Petersburg TV's independence – show that he has not changed his views. But post-coup squabbles among the democrats and the forming of new political factions may lead to jostling or control of the air either by exploiting old political structures or in Western style by manipulating market forces.

Many of the familiar faces from the democratic ranks are back on the screen, but the task ahead is awesome. The price of freedom has propelled television straight into a market economy with its own commercial and competitive pressures. Moreover, television is not starting from a healthy economic base: equipment and studio facilities are in a terrible state of decrepitude, electricity costs are becoming more expensive and reasonably priced television sets are not available. There are already gloomy forecasts that if politics doesn't kill television, the market will. Thus, while the first real chance to remodel television along democratic lines is both exciting and challenging, it is fraught with economic and political uncertainty.

Index

Television News Working Party, (TNWB), *see under* European Broadcasting Union
Television without Frontiers, 82, 97
Thatcher, Margaret, 102
Thompson, E. P., 14
TIS, *see* Trade in services
Trade in services (TIS), 96, 101, 106
Trefalt, Mito, 46–9
TSN (Television News Service), 127–8
Tsvetov, Vladimir, 118
TV Sofia (Bulgaria), 112
TV – 21st Century, 130
Twelfth Storey, 117
Twin Peaks, 47

Ufa Film und Fernseh, 60
Ulster Television, 66
UNESCO, 100–1, 104
UPITN, *see* WTN
USA
    and Europe, 97

and free trade, 95–9
overseas TV sales, 98–9
USSR, television in, 117–31, 132–3

Variety, 98
Vesti, 129
Video 9, 23
View, 117, 118, 119, 133
Visnews, 76, 83
Vosnesensky, Andrey, 120
Vremya, 125, 126–8, 133

Wallerstein, Immanuel, 105–6
Warburg, Aby, 44
Weber, Max, 2–3
Welsh-language broadcasting, 9–24
Wheel of Fortune, 46
Williams, Raymond, 14, 72
WTN, 76

Yakovlev, Yegor, 134, 135
Yanayev, Gennadi, 133
Yeltsin, Boris, 132, 133–4, 135